COUNTRY AIR

Winter and Spring

Ron Wilson

Illustrated by Isobel Norris

Farming Notes supplied by Robert Smith

First published November 1992
by
The Book Castle
12 Church Street
Dunstable
Bedfordshire
LU5 4RU

ISBN 1 871199 46 8

Computer typeset by 'Keyword', Albury, Hertfordshire.
Printed and bound by Hartnoll Ltd, Bodmin, Cornwall.

A companion volume is published: Country Air – Summer and Autumn (July 1992, ISBN 1 871199 06 9)

Front cover design incorporates a painting specially commissioned from Muriel Crossley.

CONTENTS

AUTHOR'S NOTE

We have made every effort to ensure there has been no infringement of copyright with material included in this publication. If anyone has any cause for complaint please contact the author through the publishers. We will be pleased to rectify the omission in future editions.

ACKNOWLEDGEMENTS

I am grateful to Isobel Norris for providing the delightful illustrations; to Robert Smith for his farming notes; to Muriel Crossley for the cover; to Brian Webster for reading the manuscript at short notice and for making some valuable comments and to BBC Radio Northampton for their encouragement. Any errors which remain are my own.

Ron Wilson

FOREWORD

From the rich pastureland of the Nene Valley, and the forests of Rockingham and Salcey, to the fen-like landscape of the north-east of the County – Northamptonshire typifies the rich variety of English countryside so enjoyed by those of us who reside there.

BBC Radio Northampton has recognised the importance of the countryside since it started broadcasting to the County in 1982.

Each week Ron Wilson presents 'Country Air', a thirty minute magazine of the countryside. Week by week it chronicles the seasonal changes in the countryside, explores farming attitudes and practice and focuses on the leisure and recreational use of the countryside.

This delightful book represents a marvellous 'companion' to BBC Radio Northampton's 'Country Air' programme. It's a month by month feast of information detailing traditional festivals and customs, drawing attention to flora and fauna, liberally sprinkled with apt quotations.

It's packed with a life-time's experience, knowledge and love of the countryside – a wonderful addition to the understanding and enjoyment of the landscape around us.

Nigel Dyson
Programme Organiser
BBC Radio Northampton
March 1992

ABOUT THE AUTHOR

Ron Wilson first acquired his interest in the countryside as a child in his native Norfolk. This interest developed and was reinforced whilst at teacher-training college. His love of the countryside increased when he began teaching in Cambridgeshire and later when he moved to run Everdon Field Study Centre in Northamptonshire.

When BBC Radio Northampton opened in 1982 he became involved with various programmes and now presents and produces 'Country Air' a weekly thirty minute countryside magazine.

In addition, Ron Wilson has written more than forty books including The Hedgerow Book (David and Charles), The Marshland World (Blandford), The Urban Dweller's Wildlife Companion (Blandford), Bees, Ladybirds, Spiders, Butterflies (all Young Library), Mice (A & C Black), A Year in the Countryside (Artworks), Wildflowers (Albany), Vanishing Species (Albany) and the best selling 'Back Garden Wildlife Sanctuary Book (Astragal/Penguin). Two other volumes, The Life of Plants and How the Body Works were awarded Outstanding Science Book for Children certificates by the American Science Teachers' Association.

WINTER

DECEMBER

'Shades tho yere leafless save the bramble spear
Whose weather beaten leaves of purple stain
In hardy stubborness cling all the year
To their old thorns till spring buds new again.'

John Clare

Bramble leaf

ORIGINS OF DECEMER

December used to be the tenth month, the name coming from, 'decem' which means tenth. The Romans had other names for the month. They called it 'fumosus', which means 'smokey', presumably because December can be a foggy month. The Romans also knew it as 'gelidus' which means frosty. It has had various names including Decembris and Decembre, becoming December in the 15th century.

The Anglo-Saxons had two names for December. They called it 'winter monath' and 'yule monath'. It was known as 'yule monath' because it was in December that yule logs were burnt. When the Anglo-Saxons were converted to Christianity they renamed December 'Heligh monath', which means Holy month. It was about 500 years ago that it came to be known as December. And it is in December that we have the official first day of winter on the 21st of the month. This is also the 'shortest' day in terms of daylight hours and things can only get better in the countryside as the nights get lighter.

'Cold December hath come in,
Poor people's back are clothed thin,
The trees are bare, the birds are mute,
A pot of toast would very well suit.'

INTRODUCTION

The year is rapidly drawing to a close, and if it gets very cold our wild creatures will suffer, but if it stays mild, then things should not be too bad. Even if we don't experience a cold spell our wild birds need feeding, because the amount of natural food decreases.

Although many country folk vouch that the worst of the winter is probably still to come, there are definite signs that even nature is preparing for the better days ahead. In the woods and along the roadside verges the catkins of the hazel hang like grey tassels on their leafless trees. Sometimes they hang lifeless on one of those delightfully still December days. On other days they are almost shaken from their anchorages as a bitter, and somewhat devastating wind, rips through the countryside.

BIRDS

As the month goes by the days and nights are likely to get colder. Even before the colder days arrive birds which haven't been seen in gardens since last winter will begin to reappear. Greenfinches, will soon make their way back once the nut bags are out. Apart from birds which enjoy peanuts, seed-eaters also visit the garden. And robins have their own menu: they prefer meal worms, but they eat softbill food. It is worth hanging out the bones after Sunday lunch. Birds will

Bluetit

peck at these. Even scraps can be made into useful 'cakes' and 'puddings' provided they are mixed with fat from cooking to bind the materials together. While you are cooking baked potatoes, why not put an extra one into the oven so that birds can have a treat.

Apart from the 'garden' robins many remain in woodlands, although food is less easy to find, and they often accompany visitors, as they appear and reappear on some shrub or low tree branch, especially when you stop to admire the scene. Following us around is not the robin being sociable. During their walks humans stir up the leaves, which exposes many of the small animals living there. The robin takes advantage of this activity and relishes the food which is turned over for it – and for which it hasn't had to do any work! And they are bolder than during the breeding season, almost hopping on your shoulder for a ride!

Scouring the soil

Rooks

While the weather is kind birds make the most of any food they can find. Rooks desert their nocturnal roosting sites as they go off to satisfy their voracious appetites. Soil is still being turned as massive plough shares rip into what, on the surface, appears to be a lifeless world. But rooks know that the upturned soil will expose enough food to keep them going during the coming day. Even strong winds don't seem to prevent them from being on the wing. Somewhat 'clumsy' at the best of times, they are in their element when the wind blows, using the currents to enable them to perform most masterly feats. The reason for their acrobatics at this time of the year remains something of a mystery. It is certainly not linked to courtship, since this will not occur for several months; and feeding seems to have no part to play in these airborne displays.

Welcome performance

And even the foulest of weather doesn't seem to deter that persistent, almost operatic singer, the mistle thrush. The bird hasn't been dubbed the 'storm cock' without good reason. It is strange why some birds like this are bent on defeating the elements. The louder and more blustery the wind, with its icy draught, the longer he sings and the louder and sweeter will be his song. But why should he take to the song post when all around is virtually inhospitable and most other birds are seeking shelter from the tempestuous conditions? All that can be said is that this is yet another of nature's unsolved mysteries.

> *'The bird upon the tree utters the meaning of the wind – a voice of the grass and wild flower, words of the green leaf; they speak through that slender tone',*

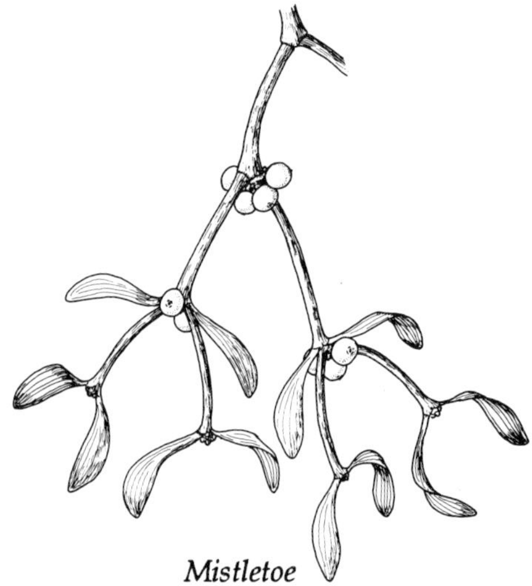

wrote Richard Jefferies about the thrush. Also known as the mistletoe thrush, because of its apparent liking for mistletoe berries. In the Mediterranean the bird feeds on the red berries of a species of mistletoe, but it has never been shown

Mistletoe

that the berries are important to it. The birds supposedly spread the seeds when they wipe their beaks on the bark of trees, which pushes the seeds into cracks where some may start to germinate. If it did feed on mistletoe it is fortunate that it has found an alternative source food supply, since mistletoe, while not extinct, is not as common as it was, say, a couple of decades ago. The mistletoe link has also been stressed by ornithologists for some time, including Thomas Bewick who commented in his British Birds that unless the seeds of mistletoe were passed through the body of the mistle thrush they would not germinate. Mistletoe grows best on apple trees, as well as poplar, and not, as many people think, oak. But old apple trees are disappearing fast and the newer varieties don't offer as much 'space' for the birds to spread their seeds – or for the mistletoe to germinate.

The mistle thrush also become more vocal at other times and you may even be woken in the 'early' hours of the morning by one of these competent songsters. The mistle thrush has innumerable alternative names including 'horse thrush', 'fen thrush', 'marble thrush' and 'gawthrush', apparently from its harsh alarm calls. It has been actively pursued by naturalists for hundreds of years. As far back as the 4th century BC Aristotle was aware of it, and made mention of it in his 'History of Animals', and the name mistle thrush, used more than a thousand years ago, is Anglo-Saxon in origin. At that time it seems both song and mistle thrush were lumped together as one species, differentiation only coming in about the eighth century when one was given the name 'song'.

Aerobatic manoeuvres

Over fields showing new growth of winter wheat, skylarks may be practising their aerobatic displays. They will come down to earth to feed, taking almost any vegetable matter they can find. If any grain is left it's readily eaten, together with weed seeds, and any frost damaged vegetables. The poet Shelley was so taken by the bird that he wrote a long poem to it, the first verse of which reads:

'Hail to thee blithe spirit!
Birds thou never wert –
That from heaven or near it
Pourest thy full heart
In profuse strains of unmeditated art'.

Their song can sometimes be heard at this time of the year, and although they are not as vocal as in the breeding season skylarks sing for most months of the year with the exception of August, and possibly July. The bird was also immortalised by an unknown 17th century poet when he penned these words:

'Brave flight of music, and a sublime song.
When wings thus sweetly fly into a tongue!'

Comings and goings

Once breeding is over skylarks tend to seek the company of their own kind and they can be seen together in flocks at this time of the year. Some birds may leave our shores: others will come from north-eastern Europe and join our own residents. However, it is generally assumed that the two groups of birds stay in separate flocks. Skylarks have also been recorded as departing our shores in autumn and winter. Whether these are British birds is not certain. Ornithologists suggest that some of the immigrants which arrive will only be passing through, although others spend the winter with us. Having fed they will set off again. It is known that within Britain those birds which inhabited upland areas will move to lower ground to avoid excessive cold and snowy conditions.

Skylark

It is probably true at this time of the year that, like the rest of the months, the skylark is the first bird to break into song first thing in the morning. The country saying 'up with the lark' is a matter of fact and not fiction, as with some country comments. The skylark has attracted the attention of many poets through the ages. In the fifteenth century William Dunbar penned these words:

'Through beamis red, gleaming, as ruby sparks,
The skyes rang for the shouting of larks'.

The Christmas bird

As the month progresses and Christmas comes nearer, there is one species which is virtually inseparable from the Christian festival, undoubtedly due to its links with folklore. The robin has been associated with the season for a very long time. He is still seen adorning innumerable Christmas cards every year. Yet, strangely it was once considered unlucky to send a Christmas card bearing a portrait of this harmless and popular bird. The superstition did not appear to last long: the Christmas card was only invented last century.

Because of its links with man during the time of the year when it doesn't have a mate and is not breeding, the robin has endeared itself to everyone. Yet, out of this period, it can be an extremely aggressive creature, fighting off its own kind, and occasionally inflicting serious injury on them. It is immortalised too in pantomime, taking an important 'role' in Babes in the Wood:

Robin

'No burial this pretty pair
From any man receives
Til robin redbreast piously
Did cover them with leaves.'

More than 300 years ago, Drayton made a similar comment about the bird which was known as the ruddock, and a quote which undoubtedly has associations with the Babes in the Wood reference.

'Covering with moss the dead's enclosed eye,
The little red-breast teaches charitie.'

Another story tells how it was the robin which was supposed to have covered our Lord's body after His death on the cross.

Warning calls

The diminutive wren is still on 'guard' as it were and will utter an alarm call should danger threaten. Dunnocks can be heard making their familiar 'wee, sissy-weeso, wee sissy-weeso' call – repeating it time and time again, apparently oblivious to the fact that no one is listening to its harmonies.

Taking evasive action

Away from the garden other birds will be searching for nourishment. The large areas of water found in many counties – reservoirs, canals, lakes, ponds, gravel pits – all attract birds. On some larger areas of water the dabchick, also known as the little grebe, still feeds. If it is disturbed or alarmed it tends to dive rather than take to the wing, re-surfacing where cover is provided by waterside vegetation. The majority of these birds seem to select sites where such protection is afforded by aquatic and marginal vegetation. But if none is available, the dabchick still dives, returning slowly to the surface. Here it remains with only the head and neck above the surface, the rest of the body concealed below the water. Its constant alertness was noticed by Shakespeare and in 'Venus and Adonis' we find:

'Upon this promise did he raise his chin
Like a dive-dapper, peering through a wave
Who being look'd on, ducks as quickly in'.

Poet Michael Drayton was much taken with the continual

diving antics of this water bird when he wrote in Poly-Olbion:

'Now up, now down again
that is hard to prove
Whether under water most
it liveth or above'.

Dabchick (in winter plumage)

Local names reflect the dabchick's diving habit – 'divedapper', 'divy duck' and 'doucker' are all examples. But it also has other interesting, if somewhat obscure names, including 'drink a penny', 'Tom puddin' and 'penny bird'.

Life becomes more difficult

Other common 'waterfowl' will be around as well. Canada geese are busy cropping the grass around the edges of reservoirs. Sometimes they fly off and take their food from a field of winter wheat. Here they can do a great deal of damage. Large flocks can be seen in and around many reservoirs.

Song thrush pulling worm from lawn

There are lots of squally conditions during December. Once the leaves have been wrenched from the hedgerow trees and shrubs, there is little comfort for the birds. They are unhappy with these conditions. Not only does it mean that they will get cold, but they are also likely to lose valuable heat – and so any stored fat will be used up as energy. To conserve body heat they seek out what shelter they can. This may be in in woods, copses and spinneys, or in thick hedges, along banks and amongst deep branches where the effect of the wind is reduced, and which provide some protection. But some remain and have periods of activity; species like blackbirds can be seen flying fast and low using the hedge as a shield for their activities. Gusty conditions in particular are difficult for birds: they cannot get the rhythm and seem to despair at times! In such conditions even the hardier song birds, like thrushes and blackbirds, will seek refuge somewhere, although this may only be temporary.

Some birds are better adapted for flying in windy conditions. Birds like the magpie use the tail to help steer it in the direction it wants to go. Other birds, like chaffinches, seem to wait for an opportune moment and then spring out of the hedge like an arrow out of a bow. But some birds, which fly with undulating movements – tits and finches, for example – will not be able to cope and tend to stay 'indoors' in these adverse situations. Most birds will try to feed – and they need to take advantage of habitats which provide shelter. Things are not too difficult for bluetits which make sorties into woods – except in the most severe conditions. In the open, they can protect themselves by feeding close to hedgerows which are not battered by the wind or in a ditch where wind blown leaves can be overturned to reveal a source of food beneath the temporary covering.

'Family' get-togethers

Large flocks of birds can be seen moving about amongst the branches of the bare trees. Members of the tit family come together at this time of the year. Usually the dominant species in any flock is the blue tit, but other members include great tits, marsh tits, long tailed tits and coal tits. From about September through to December the blue tits will be searching for food amongst rotten timber. But from about November onwards they change their tactics, turning their attention to leaf buds. Many blue tits leave the wood to relocate themselves in parks and gardens. It is interesting to watch their flight path as they move about in the garden. It is never in a straight line: some people would call their movements erratic. This is an indication of the way they behave in woodland, where the birds weave in and out of the trees – to avoid crashing into obstacles and to avoid being caught by predators.

Searching for food

At the beginning of the month there may still be plenty of hips and haws around, although in some years they have been 'attacked' by now. Flocks of fieldfares will be raiding some of the hawthorn bushes soon – and they will probably be joined by redwings. Fieldfares seem to become more alarmed than the redwings. Our own thrushes prefer to stay away from their visiting Continental cousins.

Fieldfare

In woods, woodpeckers are still busy 'tap tapping' their way along the trunks of trees as they search for food. They find plenty of larvae here to keep them well fed for some time. Down on the ground the green woodpecker is busy, and Logan Pearsall Smith wrote 'Then suddenly from the tree trunks and forest recesses comes the green woodpecker, and mocks at me with an impudent voice full of liberty and laughter.'

INSECTS

Just when you think you begin to understand the ways of nature, something comes along to put a question mark over it all. Whereas most moths have succumbed to the cold, there are one or two species which manage to get through the winter months by being active at some time. This is true as far as the winter moths are concerned. Why nature should decide that this is a good time to be active will always remain something of a mystery. The winter moth can be seen on the wing through the autumn into winter. It is the winged male which is generally encountered: the female is wingless. He can be seen fluttering almost feebly as if he can hardly cope with the tumbling winter temperatures. Lacking wings, the female relies on the male to find her. After they have mated she seeks out suitable places for egg-laying and almost any deciduous tree may suffice. Once the eggs have been laid they will remain on the tree, hatching when spring arrives. This is yet another mystery. Why be out at this time of the year to lay eggs which are going to remain 'dormant' right through the winter!

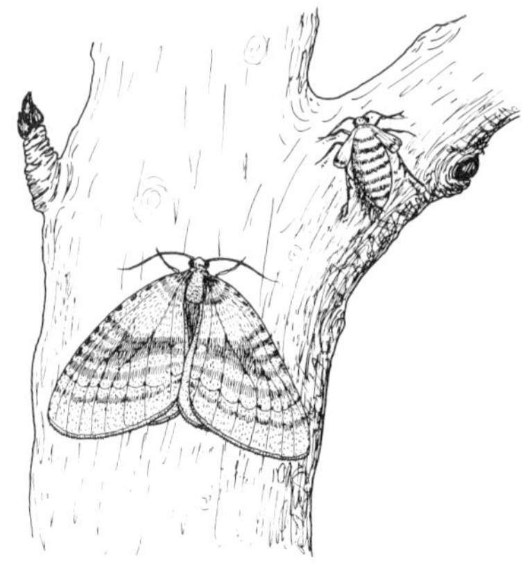

Winter moths

TREES

This is the time of the year when evergreens come into their own. When deciduous trees have all but lost their leaves, the evergreens add a touch of life to the countryside, with species like the Scots pine standing sentinel over many a forlorn landscape. Our ancestors were intrigued by these evergreens, which were seen as symbols of eternal life. And that is why when we decorate our house with evergreens we are continuing a tradition which has its origins in pagan customs. Apart from the conifers – with the exception of larch, the only British fir tree to lose its needles in autumn – the other 'popular' evergreens are the holly and the ivy, although those like the laurel and yew should not be overlooked.

Scots pine

TREE OF THE MONTH – THE YEW

One of the most intriguing evergreen species is the yew. Often encountered in churchyards it was planted there and beside houses for a purpose. The yew gave protection to those who lived in houses and those who were buried in the churchyard. It was also believed that apart from protecting the people, the church yew would also protect the church from evil and keep both the devil and evil spirits at bay. Sometimes yew leaves were scattered on the grave as the coffin was lowered, a practice which would also ensure everlasting life. But there is sometimes a less romantic, if perhaps more plausible explanation. Yew trees are one of the few species which manages to survive on the 'unpleasant secretions given off by the graves'.

The yew was important to our ancestors in other ways. It was from the trunk of the tree – and not the branches as most people assume – that the best bows were made, long before Robin Hood rose to fame, or notoriety, whichever way you choose to look at it. Bows had to be made from the straightest timber without any knots. Each trunk would probably only be able to provide enough timber for three or four bows – quite a waste of wood. Although the British yew provided many bows, it is likely that the majority of these – especially those used by English soldiers – would have been made from timber imported from the Continent. This is generally

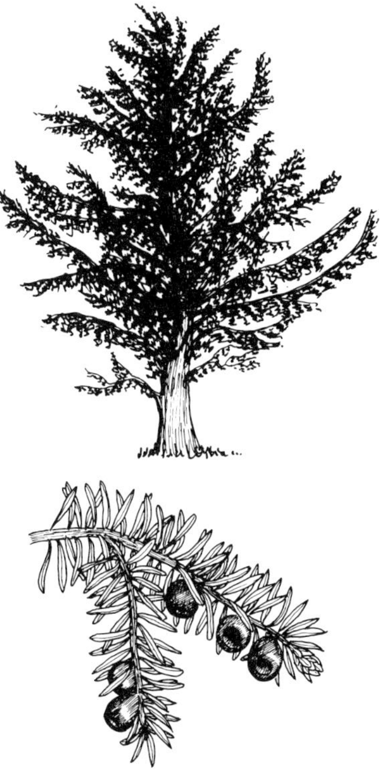

(English) Yew tree and fruits

free from the knots which are common faults in English yew trunks.

It has been suggested that the other reason for planting yew trees in churchyards was because they were safe from the ravages of cattle – which might eat the seeds within the berries which are poisonous. It is common in some churchyards to see sheep grazing these days. They are usually removed before the yew tree sports its distinctive berries.

Christmas plants

The other evergreen associated with Christmas is the holly (*Ilex aquifolium*), and although it has been suggested that the name is a corruption of 'holy' no one is certain whether this is so or not. It is more likely that it has reached us from the Anglo-Saxon 'holegn'. The *aquifolium* means 'pointed leaves'. In the past holly trees survived because our ancestors thought it was unlucky to fell the tree, since it is an evergreen – a sign of eternal life and good luck. Bunches of holly were used to 'thrash' chilblains to cure them. Holly trees are either male or female and berries will only be produced where both trees occur together, since cross-pollination has to take place. It is the female trees which ultimately produce the distinctive berries much sought after by birds as a source of food. But birds are not the only creatures which rely on the tree for food. The female holly blue butterfly lays her eggs on holly in the spring, and when they hatch the caterpillars manage to feed on the tough leaves. In autumn the larvae feed on ivy. When holly is not available the spring caterpillars feed on other plants, including bramble, gorse, dogwood and spindle.

Life goes on

Woodlands are interesting places this month. Most of the leaves will have fallen from the trees, and a thick layer of litter covers the ground. It is worth gently poking about in this. Leaf litter provides shelter and a home for a wide range of animals. And because animals seek shelter here, other creatures – the predators – will also come in search of food.

Down on the ground chaffinches utter their distinctive 'twink twink' call as they hunt for food, turning over beech leaves in search of hidden mast. There are plenty of rotting logs and these are important to wildlife. As we mentioned last month, fungi of many kinds live on and in rotting wood. Threads push into the timber speeding up the decay process. And animals live here too. Many insects lay their eggs in timber. When the eggs hatch the larvae feed on the timber, although growth is slow because wood is not particularly nutritious.

Empty bird nesting boxes attract mice – as will our houses. Long-tailed field mice, as well as yellow-necked mice, will come inside. Like the fieldfares, the wood mouse – or long tailed field mouse – enjoys haws.

WILD FLOWERS

The milder autumns we have experienced of late mean some plants will still be flowering in December. A good place to look is along the headlands which get missed by the plough – and this still happens in some fields. Amongst the species to be encountered is the scentless mayweed with its white flowers. Several species of speedwells, with their delightful blue flowers, could well be in bloom if frosts haven't killed them off. These include the green and grey field speedwells, together with the Persian speedwell. The latter is worth searching for with its delightful blue and white flowers which are held aloft on long stalks. As its name suggests it is not a native species, although related to our more familiar germander speedwell. It has been

Germander speedwell

around in Britain for around 170 years, the first record being reported in the first quarter of the 19th century.

In very mild conditions both celandines and coltsfoot may flower towards the end of the month, although the majority resist the temptation until late January or February. But with relatively few plants in flower other than those which manage to survive right through the winter – the red and white deadnettles, daisies and dandelions, as well shepherd's purse – it is worth seeking out moss plants. They can be found in a range of habitats. They seem to be just as much at home on a wall as on the woodland floor. And they will be found on roofs, on tree trunks and logs, pathways, lawns and in the gutters – almost anywhere which provides them with the moisture they need for growth and also for the dispersal of the spores.

Adapted for a difficult life

Taking a closer look, especially at those growing on walls, *Tortula muralis* is one species which is 'blossoming'. In dry conditions, when the plant might be in danger of drying up, the tongue-shaped leaves can wrap themselves around the stem. A careful examination of the plant shows that long hairs grow from the blunt tips of the leaves. It has been suggested that these help to control heat loss when conditions are less favourable. They do this by providing the rest of the moss plant with a protective shield. Mosses form two main groups. There are those which can only take water from whatever they happen to be growing on. Others, like *Tortula muralis,* have the ability to absorb water over the plant's whole surface.

Ivy-leaved toadflax colonises walls and it may still be in flower on some sunny walls, deriving its nourishment from the wall. The 'muralis' part of the plant's Latin name is a reference to its wall-growing habits. It gets its common name because the flowers are like those of toadflax, and the leaves, which bear a superficial resemblance – at least in shape – to those of ivy. In Italy it is known as 'Madonna's flower'. Although well established in many places, the plant is not a native British species, being brought from the Mediterranean in about 1640, where it was planted in rockeries. Within a short space of time the seeds 'escaped' and the plant established itself in the wild. Ivy-leaved toadflax relies on bees to bring about pollination. Once fertilized the seeds start to develop inside capsules, and when the stalk twists round these they are forced into the wall. Some seeds remain here to germinate and others may be taken by birds and insects.

One plant which was important to our ancestors was ground ivy (see March) and although the flowers faded some time ago, the plant appears to have a new lease of life at the year's end. The worn out leaves are replaced by a fresh burst of greenery which will see the plant through the winter, and presumably make it ready for vigorous growth when the warmer spring weather arrives.

Down in the water, things have been happening too. The great growth of plant life has gradually come to a standstill as plants make 'preparations' for the less favourable conditions to follow. Two of our four species of duckweeds decrease their coverage of the water surface, but both ivy duckweed and common duckweed can be seen floating on the surface through the winter. The other two species 'die' off, but before they disappear they produce special winter buds. These become heavy with stored food and sink to the bottom of a pond. By next spring some of the food store will be depleted and the plants become lighter and float back to the surface.

MAMMALS

The cold still nights of December seem to echo with the piercing sound made by courting foxes. There always seems to be competition for vixens. Once a dog fox has tracked one down, he does his best to keep her in tow – or perhaps better still keep in tow. He marks his territory rigorously, and sees off other would-be intruders. It isn't time for mating, and it may be a month or so before the pair are ready to perform this important act. During this 'stressful' time he has to ensure that he retains the interest of the vixen.

With Britain's erratic climate, the activities of mammals

during the winter may be similarly erratic. Hedgehogs wake during warmer spells, and may be out and about in search of food. During mild winters some seem to be on their rounds continuously. One of the noticeable features is that more and more are killed on the roads during these warmer winters. In days gone by hedgehogs seemed to go off to sleep for the winter and seldom wake up. Certainly the number of road casualties was much less than it is now. Bats, too, may be stirred by a warm spell. It is highly unlikely that they will find much to eat. There may be the occasional winter gnat, but for bats insect-life at this time of the year is especially sparse.

ON THE FARM

The last of the sugar beet will be lifted with the sugar beet campaign ending in January. Any sugar beet lifted but not delivered to the factory immediately must be protected from frost.

Land intended for spring crops is ploughed so that frosts can break down the soil. Where farmyard manure is produced this will be spread before being ploughed in.

Routine jobs like hedgelaying and ditching and general maintenance will be done when weather and time permits.

December is a 'short' month because of the Christmas period and is the season for Primestock Shows, like Smithfield, with animals being sold ready for Christmas.

Fresh birds can't be sold any more due to EEC regulations and farm-fresh turkeys will become a thing of the past.

SPECIAL DAYS

20 - ST. THOMAS'S EVE.

Ghosts are supposed to be freed on this day and can roam 'at will' until Christmas Eve.

21 - ST. THOMAS

was the 'doubting' apostle, and not much is known about him. House to house begging was a feature of the Saint's day, when poor women went round in search of money in a custom known as Thomassing or 'going-a-gooding'.

Another custom involved cutting an apple in half. If the number of seeds in each piece were equal then a marriage would take place in the family. Should a seed have been damaged when cutting, the relationship would not run smoothly, and two damaged seeds indicated widowhood.

24 - CHRISTMAS EVE

was the time when the large yule log was dragged into the house and placed on the kitchen hearth. The yule candle was often lit for the first time as the log was brought in. The lighted candle was placed in the centre of the dinner table and couldn't be moved or put out, being left until it went out of its own accord.

25 - CHRISTMAS DAY - THE BIRTH OF CHRIST

is now celebrated as a secular, rather than a Christian, festival by most people.

26 - ST. STEPHEN or BOXING DAY.

St. Stephen who was stoned to death is remembered on this day. Various activities used to take place, including squirrel hunting and bird shooting. Livestock were also bled, a practice which was supposed to be good for the health of horses used for hard work.

The 26th is also known as Boxing Day, from an ancient custom when boxes of food were handed round, later superseded by wrapped presents, a custom which has been replaced by the giving of gifts on Christmas Day.

'Blessed be St. Stephen, there's no fasting upon his even.'

27 - ST. JOHN

was a fisherman, and the brother of James. One of St. John the Baptists's disciples, he then followed Christ. John became Bishop of Ephesus, and he is said to have died when he was more than one hundred years old.

One saying associated with the day is 'St. John to borrow'. Farmers often borrow money on this day so that they can buy new seed. The person lending the money would look at the farmer's stocks and decide how much he should be loaned, based on how well he would do in the coming season.

31 - NEW YEAR'S EVE

has a number of customs associated with it. Perhaps the best known is one from North of the Border. Scottish folk are involved in First Footing, in which the first foot over the threshold on New Year's Day has to be a stranger carrying a green sprig, although the greenery has now been replaced by a lump of coal, a coin, and some bread, which represents warmth, wealth and plenty of food for the coming year.

In a variation, everyone in the house leaves by the back door and comes in through the front, symbolising the seeing out of the old year and the welcoming in of the new one.

WEATHER AND OTHER SAYINGS

'If its freezes on St. Thomas's Day, the price of corn will fall;
if it be mild the price will rise.'

'Whatever direction the weathercock is pointing to on St. Thomas's Day, the wind will stay there for three months.'

'A dull Christmas Day without sun is not good for the harvest.'

'If beech buds are large at Christmas the summer will be moist.'

'A green Christmas brings a full churchyard,

'A green Christmas means a good harvest in the coming year.'

'If the sun shines through the apple tree
Upon a Christmas Day
When autumn comes there will
A load of fruit display.

'In December keep yourself warm and sleep.'

JANUARY

'The sparrow too their daily guest
Is in the cottage eve at rest
And robin small and smaller wren
Are in the warm holes safe agen'
John Clare

Sparrow

ORIGINS OF JANUARY

It probably comes as no surprise to discover that the Romans named January after their two-headed God Janus. It was he who was responsible for guarding doors, entrances – and beginnings. With his two faces, Janus could look both backwards and forwards at the same time. He was the ideal god to open a new year: he could look forward to what was to come and look backwards to what had gone.

'Tis he! the twin-faced Janus comes in view;
Wild hyacinths his robe adorn,
And snowdrops, rivals of the morn.
He spurns the goat aside,
But smiles upon the new
Emerging year with pride;
And now unlocks, with agate key
The ruby gates of orient day'.

INTRODUCTION

Although January marks the opening of the year and a new beginning – with spring not that far away – our ancestors didn't quite see it that way. To the Anglo-Saxons it was 'wolf month', because now these dangerous mammals were on the prowl when there wasn't enough to eat.

The birds need regular feeding and it's especially important that they have food and water when we have cold spells, which may last for many days. You don't have to go to too much expense. Most of us have some waste from the table, and these scraps can be put in yoghurt pots and warm melted fat poured over them. The pots can be hung up or the 'puddings' turned out onto the bird table. Brown bread is also good for feed to garden bird visitors.

In spite of less activity than in the height of summer, there is still much to see in the January countryside. Although fewer flowers vie for our attention, nevertheless some species will still be around. And even though some animals are no longer active, not everything has stopped. Far from it because some of our small mammals need to work even harder at this time of the year if they are going to stay alive. The hours of daylight are shorter and birds and mammals will have less time to find their food. The habits of many birds are different during the winter: some species tend to congregate together and fly around in flocks.

BIRDS

It doesn't take much to discover that the 'better days' are not too far away. On a fine day the crows may already be busy in the treetops. The males are out to attract mates. Not only does he perform a kind of clumsy dance, but he may even produce a few chosen 'words' – which one

Carrion crow at nest

writer described as not unlike the sound of a football rattle grating high above. But if that is what modern naturalists think of the crow, an earlier 'celebrity' was kinder to them. According to tradition St Cuthbert treated crows – we don't know whether it was the hooded or carrion species – with a great deal of affection, and in his loneliness they were a constant companion accompanying him on his travels around his Farne Island home.

The carrion crow gets its name from the old English 'crawe', a reference to the bird's call. The term 'carrion' is thought to have been added in the 16th century. Given the choice, they are happy feeding on a good corpse – hence carrion – although they also take other food, including eggs and fledglings in season, as well as frogs and toads – and from time to time vegetable matter.

New voices

Starlings have rediscovered that they too have a voice. Although their trilling isn't too melodious, they may be uttering some syllables of song. But on those dull days which seem to persist for what seems like weeks on end, they are less active vocally. At this time of the year when wildlife is less conspicuous, starlings are worth keeping an eye on. They're quite comical birds, with their jaunty gait and generally 'quarrelsome' nature. Even when it would be better to concentrate on feeding, rather than seeing off their own kind, and then raiding their food supply, they can't resist a 'scrap'. The birds are troublesome on occasions. When roosting they often choose a tree where thousands of birds descend to spend the night. The sheer weight of birds, not to mention droppings, often brings about the the death of the tree. The bird has a number of local names, including starnel, sheeprack and Jacob.

Birds in wood and by water

A walk in a wood, copse or spinney later in the day once the temperature has risen will often reveal hordes of chattering, squabbling birds. To hear the call of the great tit as its almost piercing song shatters the woodland silence apart seems to suggest that better times are ahead. And during some weather conditions even 'shy' birds, like the wren, will momentarily break cover from some bedraggled hedge to cheer up the scene with their delightful songs. And then just as quickly as they emerged they are gone.

A stroll along the side of a lake, reservoir, river or stream bank is rewarding, especially where there are alder trees. The new catkins are already in position, although they are small, hard purple tassels, which bear little resemblance to the flowers they will develop into in spring and which will produce and shed pollen. On the same trees last year's black cones can be seen, and many will probably have been 'sucked dry' of their seeds, but alongside them will be new black cones containing this year's crop. A look up into the trees will often reveal the activities of one or two species of feeding birds. Redpolls and siskins can be seen in the branches as they search for a supply to eat. You may have to take a much closer look through a pair of binoculars to sort out these birds from the other finches in the branches. All will be taking advantage of the rich supply of seeds, which the alder cones hold, even though the young birds are less successful at extracting them than the more adept adults. And having the right beak adaptations they make short work of the food source. The few siskins which are resident in this country are joined for the winter by their continental cousins which reckon that our climate is better than the one they have to put up with if they stay on the continent.

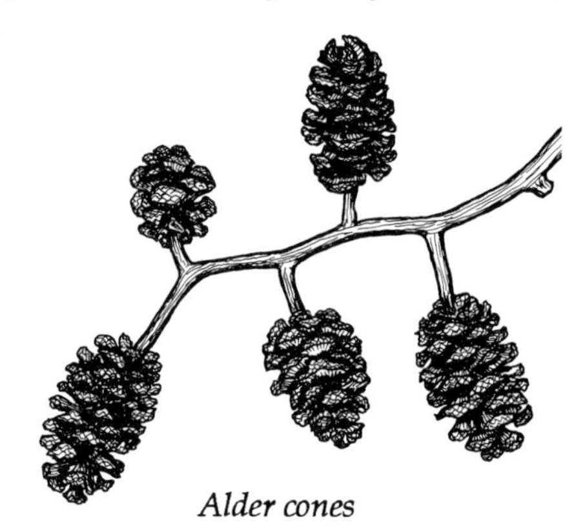
Alder cones

If redpolls are present take a closer look because these birds will be hanging upside down on the outer branches. They are seldom still for more than a few minutes – moving from one area to another as they extract any seeds left in the cones. And as Sir Oliver Heywood put it

> *'Birds are the perfect flavouring to a scene*
> *enriching its colour, and sound and character.'*

Reservoirs, sewage farms, rivers and lakes in built-up areas, as well as in the country, are worth a visit. There are plenty of birds about. Several species of gulls – black-headed are especially common – as well as waterfowl will be feeding. Additional 'migrant' mallards, tufted ducks, coots and moorhens increase the populations of any resident birds. The coots can hardly be mistaken as they spend almost as much time during this month squabbling and generally being unpleasant to each other as they are during the breeding season. In particular watch the mallards: they will be swimming around in pairs with their mates this month. The drakes – males – have already got their attractive breeding plumage, with its irridescent green feathers. They shed their dingy coats some time ago. Now they are attractive – and in complete contrast to the brown-feathered ducks – the females – which look definitely drab in comparison.

Mallard

> *'But ducks are comical things –*
> *As comical as you.*
> *Quack!*
> *They waddle round, they do'.* F W Harvey

PLANTS

As far as plants are concerned coltsfoot is an early starter and a flower which will probably show its first blooms this month, although it is likely to be seen more often in February. The golden-yellow flowers are around two and a half centimetres across. The leaves appear after the flowers and it's the shape of this part of the plant – resembling a colts foot – which gives it its name.

'Its timid leaves wait underground
So its soft stem is shawled around
To spare it from the sharp March wind'.

The Latin name is *Tussilago farfara*. The 'Tussilago' comes from the word 'tussis' which means a cough. In the past the plant was important for treating diseases of the chest. The Romans were especially fond of it for curing their chesty problems. Early folk used the leaves as a substitute for tobacco.

Stinging nettles manage to survive in even the harshest of conditions. And although they hardly burst forth into life and make great strides growth-wise, nevertheless there is life.

PLANT OF THE MONTH

One or two flowers manage to bloom through most winters except when conditions are especially trying. These include 'nondescript' species like common chickweed, shepherd's purse and groundsel. However, because there isn't much else about they are worth looking out for. Gardeners will know that groundsel manages to gain a foothold almost anywhere. It also establishes itself on other arable land as well as in waste places – in fact almost anywhere where its seeds can manage to germinate. The only difference between winter and summer flowering groundsel is that the flowers at this time of the year are smaller and the plants perhaps a little more stunted than when they are in their prime and conditions are much more favourable.

Groundsel, like so many of the other light-seeded flowers is successful because these feathery structures are transported far and wide on even the lightest of wind currents. Each seed is complete with its own parachute-like plume, a feature which ensures maximum dispersal success. Seed heads of

groundsel are reminiscent of the more familiar dandelion clock – but the groundsel is a miniature when compared with the other plant.

'Tiny green pots
With mustard tops
How fast they froth
To feathered seed.
Small birds alight
To swing and feed
On groundsel weed:
But their delight
Is gardeners' blight!'

Groundsel

Although groundsel is cosmopolitan in its tastes, winter flowering species tend to have a more restricted distribution. Many will grow in uncultivated areas of gardens and others hang on in waste sites – with more groundsel plants being seen in town than in the country. There is a good reason for this. The urban environment tends to be slightly warmer in the winter than open countryside. Groundsel gets its name from the old English 'grundeswilige' – the groundswallower! In 1538 Turner called it 'grundeswell' and 'grunswell'. In a 'Book of Simples' published in 1562 by Bullein, he said of the groundsel '... the flower of this herbe, hath whyte hayre, and when the wynde bloweth it awaye, then it appeareth like a bald headded man, therefore it is called Senecio'. It is thought that Senecio may be a corruption of the Latin 'senex', which means an 'old man'. The second part of its Latin name – 'vulgaris' implies almost that – an everyday species. When food is short at this time of the year country folk will collect groundsel to feed to their rabbits – and cage birds are partial to the leaves.

Winter survivors

And one of the other plants which survives the onslaughts of many a winter is the equally rampant, but also equally dull, shepherd's purse. Like groundsel it is a successful weed of both waste and cultivated ground. The plant gets the 'purse' part of its name from the seed pods which are shaped like a purse, and according to some experts they closely resemble the purses which can be discovered in sixteenth century paintings by Breugel – like 'Dance of the Peasants'. A closer inspection of the seed pods shows that they are flat and heart-shaped. And the shepherd's part of the name comes from the fact that the purse is on a small and not very flamboyant plant.

Shepherds purse

Shepherds, too, were poor people, hence the name. In a children's game, a child egged on another to pick the seed pods of shepherds purse. As the seeds fell out, the child who had suggested the incident would chant:

'Pick pocket, penny nail
Put the rogue in the jail'.

And there is also another game played by children in the past. These heart-shaped seed cases break – and because of this the plant was called 'mother's heart'. One child would ask another to pick a seed case and then, as the seeds dispersed, taunt the other child that in doing this he/she had broken his/her mother's heart.

In winter when there are few insects to bring about pollination this is no problem to the shepherd's purse: it doesn't need them because its flowers are self pollinated. Because of this the shepherd's purse is an opportunist and during the last Ice Age it was able to spread to new areas, since it didn't need insects to help it.

Our ancestors looked to the plant for its curative properties and it was supposed to be useful for checking nosebleeds, as well as being used as a compress on both open cuts and sores. The plant has also been found to contain a number of active ingredients, including choline, not to mention traces of tannin and resin.

Yet another dull-coloured plant will be struggling for survival this month. This is the common chickweed, its small and insignificant flowers are easily overlooked. When little other food may be about chickweed provide some birds with a tasty morsel - and the woodpigeon makes a meal of it. Like shepherd's purse it is self pollinated and can survive at this time of the year when insects are in hibernation. According to Coles writing in 'Adam and Eden' in 1657, chickens and birds love to pick the seeds, hence its name. And Gerard remarked that little birds in cages were 'refreshed by it'. Chickweed was collected in the past for salads, and also an ingredient in an ointment used to treat dermatitis.

In most Januarys the dandelion manages to bloom, and as John Tabb put it:

'With locks of gold today;
Tomorrow silver-grey;
Then blossom-bald. Behold
O man, thy fortune told'.

Early growth

In warm weather some other plants may put in an appearance. The shoots of the wild arum - lords and ladies, cuckoo pint, jack in the pulpit - call it what you will - and there are some rude names for the plant - will often be poking through the soil.

Towards the end of the month the first snowdrops are likely to appear. Having been 'struggling' under the soil for some time they have thrown up their green leaves and now the first flowers burst forth. The distinctive snow-white blooms add another dimension to the countryside this month.

TREES AND HEDGEROWS

Trees are worth more investigations too and in some mild winters, hazel catkins, continue to develop well in January. They will have their supply of pollen a bit later. Catkins are on other trees, apart from hazel and alder, like the silver birch and willow and they make some headway in January. The variety of bud form on these and other trees is worth looking at. Many are so distinctive at this time of the year that they cannot be mistaken. The red colour of the lime is in contrast to the finger like projections of the beech. Added to these are the unmistakeable black velvet-like buds of the ash and the sticky ones of the horsechestnut.

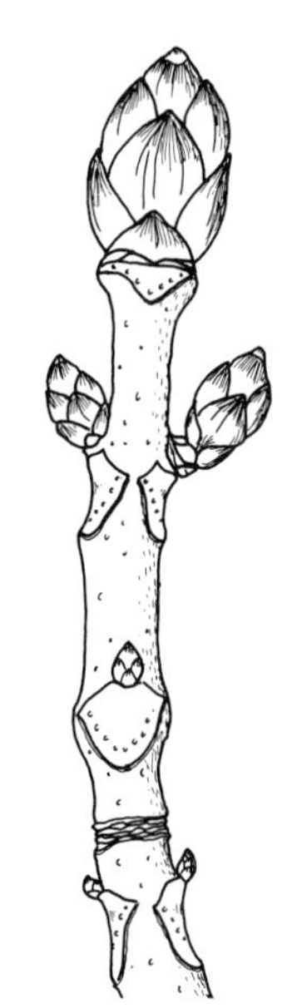

Horsechestnut buds

INSECTS

Insects are often drawn out during mild spells. One small creature which is active, although out of sight, is the earwig. Most mated in the autumn, and when the first cold snap arrived a winter home was selected. Most earwigs find logs and stones suitable and they crawl into hollowed out spaces to spend the winter. Such places may be home to large numbers of earwigs as they are not averse to sharing their winter home with their own kind. Apart from spaces under stones and logs, earwigs also go into hollow canes, other small crevices and plant stems during the hours of daylight and the colder months of winter. During this season female earwigs lay their eggs. Unlike most insects which abandon them, the earwig is a good mother. She will fuss over the eggs, checking them regularly and licking them to prevent mould

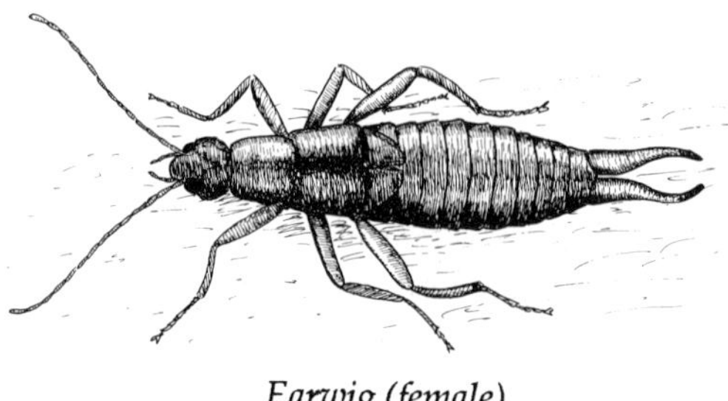

Earwig (female)

from developing: she will continue her chores until the eggs hatch in spring, and even then her maternal care is not yet over.

The pincers, so distinctive in the male, have long caused debates to rage far and wide. Some suggest that they may be used for capturing food, but this seems remote since the female doesn't have the same appendages. The insect has quite large wings, which are of tissue- like fragilty. Although few people witness earwigs in flight, they are capable of getting airborne. The supposition by some people that the word earwig, has been corrupted from the term 'ear wing' is highly unlikely. It has also been suggested that those 'menacing' pincers might be used for folding away the wings, another topic which causes many an argument amongst naturalists. The most plausible explanation is that they have some 'sexual' purpose and may even be used in combat.

There is yet another explanation for the strange name. And that is that these creatures entered people's ears – causing a few problems. That these small insects would do this now is highly unlikely, but in the days when the floor was the bed this was more likely. The human ear would have provided a warm sanctuary, especially in the colder months of the year. This belief is held across Europe as well as in the British Isles. The French call it 'ear piercer' and the Germans the 'ear worm'.

MAMMALS

When much else in the countryside seems to be less active there is one creature which seems always to be on the move. Almost anywhere you go the mole has 'been at it'. In some places whole fields appear to be ploughed by this energetic and hard-working mammal – often much to the annoyance of the farmer. Grass verges come under attack too, as does the lawn. It is only in very cold weather that the mole finds it more difficult to operate. Then the small velvet-coated mammal will go further down into the soil – where life is easier both for digging and for catching food.

'He wears a coat of velvet fine
Coloured black as ink.
His tiny eyes can hardly see
His little nose of pink'.

Reg Scarfe

The piles of soil – mole hills – which give away the creature's activities are important to birds. Take a close look at many and they have been 'flattened'. Birds will search them for any creatures – food – which has been turned up. Fresh spoil heaps are quickly investigated in many areas.

Mole

High in the trees

The dreys which grey squirrels have high up in the trees are much easier to spot at this time of the year. These 'delighful' mammals, which attract the attention of young and old, are often a nuisance in afforested areas, where they can do a great deal of damage. But that apart it is the time of the year when the first grey squirrels will give birth to their first litter of the year. With woods much quieter at this time, squirrels may be seen – and often heard. Its distinctive churring noise reveals its presence. This is an aggressive act, as they scold and chase off would-be intruders.

January is the month too when a large mammal makes its presence felt. Foxes seek mates this month and their almost blood-curdling screams echo around some parts of the countryside. When the countryside has a covering of snow and there has been a sharp frost coating everything with a white crust, it is a good time to look for the fox. Here and there footprints can be followed. Although foxes will be out and about during the day in some areas, they are nocturnal by

Red fox

nature. The reason for their nocturnal jaunts is that the food which they need will also be on its rounds at the same time. If you do a bit of detective work and follow the tracks it is often possible to glean vital information from the mammal's previous night's activities. You can see areas where the fox began to dig the soil in pursuit of some small mammal like a vole. Seeking shelter in its tunnel this small mammal may have escaped the fox's attention. But very little is safe when the fox is hungry – and in some cases where it hasn't done too well a whole series of clues can be discovered along its trail. At this time of the year with the first lambs in the field the fox may find a larger meal. There are conflicting views about which lambs the fox will take. Some experts suggest it is only weaker ones; others that it can be healthy lambs not too well protected by their mothers.

Death in winter

As with many creatures winter is a trying time for foxes. Many will meet their deaths on roads, just as they do at other times of the year. Younger, less well nourished 'cubs' – which now lead an independent life – can be in danger. With the fox population at least double and possibly treble that of last autumn, there can be some competition. It is difficult to determine how many will die, because numbers are not known. Few will succumb to starvation: most will be killed in a variety of ways. Some farmers will endeavour to kill off those they think are a problem to their sheep; the brightly attired gentlemen on their horses may account for others; some are trapped for their pelts and gamekeepers may dispense with some if they think their birds are at risk. A few, and again the number is not known, will be targetted by public health officials who feel they may be a hazard to the community at large. Yet in spite of this the fox population seems relatively stable.

In theory – and without any threats – a fox can live for anything up to ten years. But few of last year's cubs will reach that ripe old age. It is reckoned that the majority of those born last year will be dead before the end of the first winter. And for those that survive, longevity is hardly likely: most die before they make their fourth birthday. In remoter areas where humans have little effect, older foxes can be found. How young foxes break the ties with their parents is not really understood. It is thought that they may leave around autumn, although there are hangers on – not unlike the human family! Perhaps they go further afield in search of extra food, and then sleep away from the family home. Or maybe the parents ensure that they are 'kicked' out' before the winter. This will ensure that no two foxes are competing in the same area for food.

Tracks in snow (fox and rabbit)

Although winter is a 'bad' time to be out in the countryside at night, it is also the best time to investigate the many calls which foxes make. These mammals have a complex means of communicating with others of their ilk. Although foxes 'call' throughout the year it is during the winter that they make the most 'noise'. The 'scream' is the sound most associated with the vixen, although the dog also emits the same sound less frequently. It is the 'wow wow wow' which the dog makes which echoes eerily around a winter woodland in the still of the night.

January, often a bleak month, has much variety to offer the wildlife observer.

ON THE FARM

Cows are milked twice each day and will receive supplementary concentrated food while in the milking parlour. Chickens are kept for meat and eggs. Pork and bacon are produced by both indoor and outdoor pig units. Where beef cattle are kept they will be sent to market from the fields in summer and from the yards in winter. Although certain crops will be treated with fertilisers, weedkillers and fungicides at suitable stages of development, spraying is often an on-going process, depending on the stage of growth and pest problems. Indoor plants and flowers, as well as salad crops are produced throughout the year by market gardeners.

Farming activities have changed over the years. In the not so distant past repairs of machinery and general maintenance had to be done in January when it wasn't possible to get on the land. The farm labourer was a versatile person, and carried out such jobs as hedgelaying and ditching. In many places ditches are no longer needed as the water is piped away, and where they still exist machines are used to clean them out. Although many hedges are now cut mechanically, hedgelaying is coming back in some parts of the country.

Potatoes harvested in the autumn need to be sorted before they are sold and, although modern machinery has replaced the old-fashioned potato riddle, this operation is still carried out on many farms.

As far as livestock is concerned, the first of the lambs will be born this month, and store lambs from the previous year will be fattened on kale and turnips. After the 1 January they are not called lambs – but teggs in Northamptonshire – and hoggets in other places. Dairy cows and beef cattle which are still indoors for the winter are being fed on silage and additional feeds. Pigs are a problem, especially outdoor ones when the weather is wet.

In the 'old days' farm manure would have been spread and ploughed in, but this isn't likely to happen on modern farms since most crops will have been planted in the autumn.

During this and next month farmers will have problems from pigeon damage if the land is not covered with snow. Crops like oilseed rape are especially vulnerable.

Where fruit farming is part of the scene, orchards will be pruned this month.

SPECIAL DAYS

1 – NEW YEAR'S DAY.

To mark the New Year parties are held and people sit up to see the old year out and the new year in. In some places the door is actually opened so that the old year can escape to allow the new year space. It has long been the custom to sing 'Auld Lang Syne' at the stroke of midnight. And this is the day on which resolutions are made – and undoubtedly as many broken. According to the American writer Benjamin Franklin:

'With the old almanack and the old year
Leave thy old vices, tho' ever so dear.'

6 – FEAST OF THE EPIPHANY.

The word 'Epiphany' means 'showing forth' because it was on this day that the three wise men came to see Jesus. In Spain children leave their shoes on the window sills filled with straw for the camels of the Wise Men. The straw is taken and replaced with small gifts.

January 6 also marks Twelfth Night. According to tradition Christmas festivities come to an end, and all the decorations in the house have to be taken down. Some folk used to eat a mince pie on each of the days leading up to Twelfth Night to ensure twelve happy and prosperous months.

It has often been suggested that our peasant forebears had twelve days holiday at Christmas in the hard dark days of past centuries. It is true that although certain chores had to be performed on the 'farm', this was a time when not much was happening on the land. Today, many of the traditional tasks of the countryside have disappeared. Hedging and ditching, important features of the farm before the advent of machinery, were temporarily suspended during the twelve days of Christmas. Twelfth Night was so important - and to many of our ancestors so exuberant - that it was thought necessary to appoint a King of Misrule. He was there to give the festivities and jollifications some form of respectability.

7 - PLOUGH MONDAY.

Our ancestors used to celebrate the day after Twelfth Night as Plough Monday. This was the day when the festivities really came to an end in no uncertain fashion and the labourers had to return to the grind. Working women also returned to their work, and to them it was St Distaff's Day - a distaff was another word for spindle.

The corn dolly - or kern baby - which had occupied a prominent position in many farm houses was also the focus of attention on Plough Monday. The symbolic straw-woven object was taken from its resting place and carried to the first furrow to be turned, and it was ceremoniously placed in the ground, so that the plough would bury it. Inside the 'womb' of the earth she was able to perform her annual miracle which would make the seed grow and produce a good crop of grain.

WEATHER AND OTHER SAYINGS

As far as the weather is concerned January is an unpredictable month. Sometimes there are heavy snowfalls and extremely low temperatures. Yet these severe conditions may alternate with periods when the temperature reaches the fifties. According to an old proverb, 'Winter weather and women's thoughts often change' – and some people have used this to describe January's mood weather-wise.

'If there are clouds on St. Ananias's Day (25) then floods are likely.'

'If on St. Vincent's day the sky be clear
More wine than water will crown the year.'

'Remember St. Vincent's Day
If the sun his beams display
Be sure to mark the transient beam
For 'tis a token bright and clear
Of prosperous weather all the year.'

28 January is St. Paul's Day

'If St. Paul's Day be fair and clear
It doth betide a happy year
But if it change to snow or rain
Then will be dear all kinds of grain
If clouds and mist do dark the sky
Great stores of beasts and birds will die
And if the winds do fly aloft
Then war shall vex the kingdom oft.'

'The blackest month of all the year
Is the month of Janiveer.'

'If the grass grows in January
It grows the worse for all the year'.

'A January spring is worth nothing.'

'If the birds begin to sing in January,
frosts are on the way.'

'March in January
January in March.'

'March in Janiveer
Janiveer in March, I fear.'

'Under water dearyhth
Under snow bread.'

'If January calends be summerly gay
Twill be winterly weather till calends of May.'

'Janiveer
Freeze the pot upon the fire.'

'As the day lengthens
The cold strengthens.'

FEBRUARY

'The hedgehog from its hollow roo
Sees the wood moss clear of snow
And hunts each hedge for fallen fruit
Crab hip and winter bitten sloe.'
John Clare

Crab apples

ORIGINS OF FEBRUARY

For the Romans the fifteenth of February was important. It was their feast of Februa, the word which gives it name to the month. The name of the feast comes from the word februare, which means 'to purify'. This was the feast of purification and cleansing, appropriate after the long cold days of winter.

INTRODUCTION

February can be a 'difficult' month in the countryside. On some days the temperature soars to around the fifties and on others it may plummet to well below freezing, with snow and frost affecting 'normal' life and activities

As we move towards the end of winter, life is becoming very difficult for our wildlife and especially in severe bouts of weather. In the wood creatures are searching desperately for food. In mild Februarys that is not so much of a problem because they can get food more easily by poking amongst the leaf litter and pulling earthworms from the soil. But prolonged frosts drive the earthworms well below ground and with a solid covering to the landscape, finding food becomes something of a nightmare.

BUTTERFLIES AND OTHER INSECTS

On delightfully warm days hibernating butterflies may be tempted out as the 'winter' weather goes haywire, and temperatures soar towards the 50F (11°C) mark. Small tortoiseshells and peacocks may be stirred by the warmth and be seen on the wing.

Other insects may be out too, and the honeybees may make their first tentative excursions from the hive. Winter flowers will provide them with a much needed top up of energy, and species like the heliotrope will offer welcome sustenance. Sometimes it is possible to see 'intruders' flying around with the bees. The most likely imposter is a hoverfly, which rejoices in the Latin name of *Eristasis tenax*. Only close observation will reveal that the hoverfly is not a true bee. In colour it is almost indistinguishable from them: a true mimic – except, unlike the bees, it only has one pair of large wings, compared to the two pairs which the bees possess. The habits of this particular species of hoverfly are not particularly savoury. The female places the eggs in 'smelly' places, like farmyard drains or stagnant water in ditches. It is not surprising that in these conditions the insect needs fresh air, which it obtains by thrusting a long breathing tube up to, and through the surface film. This is the reason why the larva is more popularly known as the 'rat-tailed maggot'. This is the species which survives in polluted water, when most other creatures have long since left – or been killed by the poisons.

Hoverfly

Bygone explanations

It is always interesting to discover what earlier 'naturalists' thought about some creatures. As far as the bee was concerned they found it more difficult to study – and they suggested that it was 'created from the body of a dead animal'. You only have to look at a tin of a famous brand of syrup to discover that bees are emerging from a lion's corpse – and accompanying the drawing is a quotation from the Bible, where Samson says 'Out of the strong came forth sweetness'. These insects may have to take evasive action should the warm spell not last. Bees will return to their hives: the hoverflies may manage to find a sheltered site, but more than likely many will perish if conditions become severe.

ANIMAL OF THE MONTH – THE BURYING BEETLE

Death comes often in the dark days of winter. Corpses would litter the countryside if it wasn't for the work of one group of insects known as the 'sexton' or burying beetles. 'Sexton' is a reference to the church official whose jobs included digging graves. And as if this wasn't enough, the insect's Latin name of Necrophorus also means 'grave-digger'! Dead bodies are important to the creatures. Not only do they provide them with a source of food, but also food for the larvae, the eggs of which are laid in rotting flesh.

Once a carcase is discovered it is fairly quickly despatched. The mode of operation varies. If the carcase is quite small, like that of a sparrow or a shrew, then the burial is performed by a pair of insects. The

Burying (Sexton) Beetles

first to arrive may have to defend its right to perform the activity and keep away others which may try to effect a take-over bid. However, as soon as a member of the opposite sex puts in an appearance, the burying beetle welcomes his opposite number with 'delight'. Should the onslaughts continue, then together the pair will continue to repel invaders. Sometimes the first beetles are driven off, but eventually a pair take control and sets to work to bury the corpse.

Should the dead body be much larger, as in the case of a rabbit or stoat, then there is no dispute as the several burying beetles which arrive to feed on the flesh are allowed to stay. Often these burying beetles are not the first visitors. Flies may have appeared, eggs been laid, and maggots hatched. This proves no problem to the burying beetles: they simply devour the maggots as well, as was noticed in 1830 by an earlier naturalist, who recorded his observations. He said that the beetles had 'established a sort of encampment about thirty inches from the carcase, to which each individual ever and anon made a raid and captured a fine fat maggot, which he bore off writhing and wriggling in his mandibles to the camping ground where it was speedily devoured'.

The burial begins! The beetles start to dig under the body, and at the same time, they remove the skin. Eventually the carcase is covered. Where corpses have purposely been tied up – either with string or wire – the beetles have dealt with the problem. When wire was attached to a limb, the beetles simply removed the limb! When it was string, they bit through it. Digging is effected when the insects use their strong front legs and flat heads to make a hole in soil. The burial chamber is big enough to take the creature and to enable the insects to move about. There are times when corpses occur on difficult ground. When this happens it is not unusual for the beetles to take the dead animal to a more suitable site so that they can dig the soil.

Once the corpse is 'underground', the male beetle leaves,

the pair having mated before he departs. It is then the task of the female to produce a place to lay her eggs. She makes a tunnel from the carrion, along which she makes small excavations. In these she lays a single egg, producing around 14 or 15 altogether. Having completed this important activity, she goes back to the corpse and feeds from the top, leaving a small hole. Five days later the larvae emerge from the eggs, and make their way along the tunnel, up the corpse, and into the hole made by the female. The female is still there, and she provides them with their first meals. The larvae are persistent and may even climb over her. She produces a brown liquid, and she opens her jaws, releases a single drop, ensuring that all larvae receive the same amount of nourishment. Within a few hours the larvae are capable of taking their own food. But their dependence on the female is not over. They return to her for feeding when they shed their first and second skins. The female will eventually leave the chamber before the larvae are fully grown. When they reach this state, they burrow away from the corpse, and change into a pupa, from which the adult will emerge in a couple of weeks.

AMPHIBIANS

Although we probably don't realise it frogs – and perhaps toads – will leave their winter quarters and go out in search of a place to breed. They will often return to the same site year after year, and with many ponds being filled in, there are fewer breeding places for them. This is why they are in decline. They have had to move to artificial ponds, particularly ornamental garden ones. These amphibians – a word which means 'double life – are found in both towns and country areas. If conditions are severe the breeding season will be delayed, but there is usually spawn in some ponds towards the end of this month. Garden ponds have become something of a lifeline in recent years, and many new ones are quickly colonised.

Frogs

BIRDS

In spite of the fact that it is still very cold for most of us some birds will have taken the plunge and mated, and be busy nest-building. One of the first to do this is the mistle thrush. Once the nest has been built, the eggs will be laid towards the end of the month. Some birds which attempt to get in on the act early may suffer if there are severe conditions, and the eggs may become frozen.

Like so many of our other birds, the mistle thrush was a woodland species. But as more and more woodland has disappeared they have had to change their lifestyle. Some 450 years ago they started moving out from woodland to establish themselves in more open terrain, with others seeking homes in both urban and rural environments. With trees in most built up areas, the mistle thrush has a place for its nest and a home for its fledglings. Parks provide breeding sites as do trees on the edges of built up areas.

Courting time

Collared doves will be courting. They were first recorded in 1953 in the Norfolk coastal town of Cromer, breeding two years later. Now they are (almost) everywhere, having taken a liking particularly to town sites.

Collared dove

Rooks will be actively repairing their nests ready for the breeding season, although some will probably have started the operation in January – and even in mild Decembers. They hold noisy 'meetings' as they go about their tasks. These meetings have come to be known as 'rook parliaments'. They seem to take more time to get started in the morning – and they will be in the rookeries for longer periods

Rook nest in treetop

before they fly off in search of food. In the past you could have seen them repairing their nests almost everywhere, but town rookeries are much less common than they used to be.

Another black bird which can hardly be mistaken is the blackbird. In cold conditions several of them will appear on one patch. I am amazed that they spend so much time and energy to get rid of would-be competitors. These avian punch-ups are quite alarming, with one blackbird setting into another with vigour. The search for food is abandoned for a short while, during which time the supply often disappears as other species take their share! The attitude changes while the blackbird is in its territory. You can watch them flying at their enemies. Then when they reach the boundaries of the territory, they take up the threat display. The defender will fan its tail, and raise its beak into the air. Sometimes the resultant fisticuffs take place on the ground; sometimes the birds fly into the air as they attack each other. There is something of opposites here too. One minute the blackbird seems to be trilling sweetly, if somewhat softly, to itself as it sits on a prominent position on a hedge or on the ground somewhere. Then the next minute it is having an affray with another of its kind.

The singing yellowhammer

As the month goes by the familiar 'little bit of bread and no cheese' becomes more noticeable, as the yellowhammer is heard more often. This, and other species, will swell the countryside choir, as they tune up again after their winter silence. In spite of perhaps some less than favourable weather, birds seem encouraged by the warmer days. The tits will be looking for suitable nesting sites, perhaps to ensure that they get the best house-building 'plots' before their relatives also take up the search.

WILD FLOWERS

A few flowers manage to brave the weather and the glowing yellow blooms of some, like the winter aconite, whose flower is bedecked with a distinctive green ruff of deeply-divided leaves, may have appeared towards the end of January. That ruff is not made up of true leaves: these will appear when the flowers have faded, and they are poisonous. The aconite will be closed in dull weather and opens up when it is bright.

'Pink elbow thrust
Through winter crust
Green lamp tipped up
Reveals gold cup.
Welcome bright light
Of aconite!'

Winter Aconite

They will be joined by the celandine, which is also a member of the buttercup family. The celandine, grows in woods and along hedgerows and hedgebanks. The leaves are distinctive and heart-shaped.

Overcoming difficulties

For many plants this is still a difficult time of the year, with soil temperatures rather on the low side. The only way plants can be sure of making headway is to have enough stored food. Early flowering species usually have a bulb below the surface which contains a store of food. Other plants survive because they have what can best be termed 'frost-proof' structures containing sufficient reserves of food. Their growth does not rely too much on soil temperatures. This is true of the snowdrop which has a bulb, providing it with enough stored food to get it started, and coltsfoot which has a thick white rhizome well buried below the surface.

Whiter than snow

Some snowdrops will have made their debut in January, but according to the saying this is the month for those 'fair maids of February'. If there is snow on the ground during February snowdrops grow longer stalks so that they can push up through the winter covering. There are those people who are so dedicated to the snowdrop that they collect the different varieties. Such collectors are known as Galanthophiles - a name which comes from part of the plant's Latin name - 'galanthus'. Like most of our common species, the snowdrop has many country names in different parts of the British Isles. Somerset folk call it Eve's tears, snowdroppers or dingle bells, while in Gloucestershire it's known as Candlemas bells, a reference to the special day which falls in February.

'The snowdrop in purest white
array
First rears its head on
Candlemas Day.'

Snowdrops

It is interesting that the word 'snowdrop' doesn't seem to have entered the vocabulary until the late 17th century. According to Gerard's herbal it was known as 'Timely flowring Bulbus violet'. In his 'Garden Book' published in 1659, Sir Thomas Hammer described the snowdrop as 'the early white, whose pretty pearl white bellflowers are tipte with a fine greene, and hang downe their heads'. In Shropshire, Derbyshire, Staffordshire, Sussex and Worcestershire they were known as 'death's flower' because their hanging flowers signified death. To some people the flower represented a 'corpse in its shroud'. Any deaths which happened in February were always blamed on the snowdrop. Another superstition held that if the snowdrop was taken into a house the eggs which hens were sitting on would not hatch. It was also said to affect the colour of butter made from milk where snowdrops had been taken into the cowshed.

William and Dorothy Wordsworth were much taken with

the flower so much so that they planted it in the orchard in Dove Cottage. How much they enjoyed these early harbingers of spring is recorded in a poem which was penned in 1803.

'Who fancied what a pretty sight
This rock would be if edged around
With living snowdrops?, Circlet bright;
How glorious to this orchard ground!
Who loved the little rock, and set
Upon its head this coronet?'

The flower's origins

There is a charming story which explains how the snowdrop came into being. When Adam and Eve were sent away from the Garden of Eden summer vanished and winter was soon upon the evicted couple. Eve did not know what to do – she could not cope with the cold. And she made the decision that if she was always going to have to live in a cold world then she would rather die. Seeing her state an angel took pity on Eve and as some of the snowflakes fell to the ground she breathed on them. Each one changed into a snowdrop, an indication that winter would not last for ever – and spring would breathe its new invigorating life into the countryside.

An alien in our midst

The flowers of the lesser periwinkle, often up to 2.5 inches across, and bluish-purple or perhaps white in colour, will usually show themselves this month. One writer described the foliage as 'Shining trails of polished leaves'. The plant thrives in hedgebanks, woodland spinneys and copses. It was thought to have been brought from warmer parts of the world and was noted by the herbalist William Turner in the middle of the 16th century. It doesn't usually produce ripe seeds, but it spreads effectively by its stems, which root when they touch the ground. In days gone by the flowers had a poignant use. Crowns or garlands were made from the flowers and placed around the heads and necks of those about to be executed.

Although this may seem strange at first, it isn't quite so outrageous, because the evergreen nature of the plant – like so many other evergreens – represented immortality. But it wasn't just those who were about to be executed who might have found a use for the plant. Apparently herbalists swore by its value in 'staunching the flow of blood' particularly from nosebleeds. In the words of one 17th century writer, 'It has an excellent virtue to staunch bleeding at the nose in Christians if made into a garland and hung about the neck'. Why you had to be a Christian to avail yourself of its properties is not really known!

A 'useless' plant

Most of the early flowers are relatively bright and easily noticeable. But that can hardly be said for the dog's mercury which may start to flower this month. According to legend it was given the name 'mercury' after the Roman god of trade, who is supposed to have discovered it. The 'dog' part of its name was attached to the plant in the Middle Ages. It was seen as worthless – and worthless objects were often given the name of 'dog' – because it was of no use to anyone else.

Unlike other plants of the countryside which have their uses, the herbalist Culpeper remarked of dog's mercury, 'There is not a more fatal plant, native of our country, than this'. An easily spotted plant early in the year, it is widely distributed in hedgebanks and woodlands, and has inconspicuous greenish flowers. Male flowers appear on one plant; female flowers on a separate one. Farmers make every effort to ensure that dog's mercury doesn't grow where there are cattle. If eaten by the

Dog's Mercury

animals it causes enteritis and produces a slimey yellow milk. The plant's presence is often discovered before encountering the species itself. This is because it gives off a unique smell, one of nature's ploys to ensure fertilzation. The smell attracts midges, and as they crawl over the female flowers they deposit pollen which they have picked up from nearby male flowers.

TREES AND SHRUBS

Larger plants are worth investigating this month, especially in woods. Many clumps of honeysuckle have had leaves since the beginning of the year. In fact some plants have them throughout mild winters. More are appearing as the weather warms up. Elder, too, is another early species to come into leaf. There is no mistaking the leaves of this shrub when you crush them between your fingers. But their appearance may be premature and they are often 'crippled' and blackened by severe frosts.

Providing a 'home'

It is worth looking at old elder stems because they support an interesting fungus. Known as 'ear fungus', the plant resembles an ear. It is worth feeling it – and if there is plenty then you could try cooking it, because it is quite a delicacy! But Europeans haven't taken to it in the same way as our far eastern cousins. It is considered such a gastronomic delicacy in that part of the world that species are especially cultivated for the table. Frost tends to play havoc with the fungus, but its growth isn't confined to late winter and early spring and you will find it growing at other times of the year. The maximum size is about 10cm.

Ear fungus on Elder

Although the ear fungus belongs to the same group as mushrooms and toadstools it is seldom compared to them. Species like ear fungus have come to be known as 'jelly fungus' because of the jelly-like feel to them. This is true when they are moist, but they become rock hard in dry conditions, which may make identification difficult. The fungus is generally associated with dead elder, although it does occur on elm. It is rare to find just one – usually there are a number.

Take a look at the alder tree which is closely related to the birch, and compare last month's catkins with those in February and you will find that they are making good headway, as are those on several other tree species, including willow and hazel. These have been on the tree since last autumn and have 'spurts' of growth in mild spells. As they continue to expand they eventually take on a delightful purple colour. The female catkins are egg-shaped and purple. Any remaining seeds will be eagerly taken by birds such as redpolls and siskins.

The buds had their uses in the past, and were collected during the cold, damp weather, just before they were about to open, and were then dried carefully. A tea was made from these, and drunk when a person rose in the morning. It was supposed to help relieve the pain of those suffering from rheumatism.

LIFE IN WATER

Even though things are beginning to stir, the February countryside is still something of a dead place. One area which is overlooked during these cold times is the water. Yet beneath the surface – with perhaps a thick coating of ice – life goes on. Any sheet ice may seal the surface for days on end – even for weeks in some severe conditions. But death does not come easily to the creatures below the surface. The animals which live there permanently are cold-blooded, a feature which helps them to survive. In simple terms this means that the temperature of their body varies to match the temperature of their surroundings – and that is why some cold-blooded creatures, like frogs and toads, hibernate. If they didn't they would not survive the punishing winter conditions. As the temperatures see-saw, water creatures will have the same happening to their bodies.

As the temperatures begin to fall each autumn many species take a dive. They move from the active water environment to the more sluggish and better protection of the mud at the bottom of the pond, lake or river. Here the nymphs of mayflies, stoneflies, alderflies and caddis and midges will survive. Although the adults of the spectacular dragonflies die in the autumn, the larvae cling to life in the bottom mud, protected from the harsher condition some way above them.

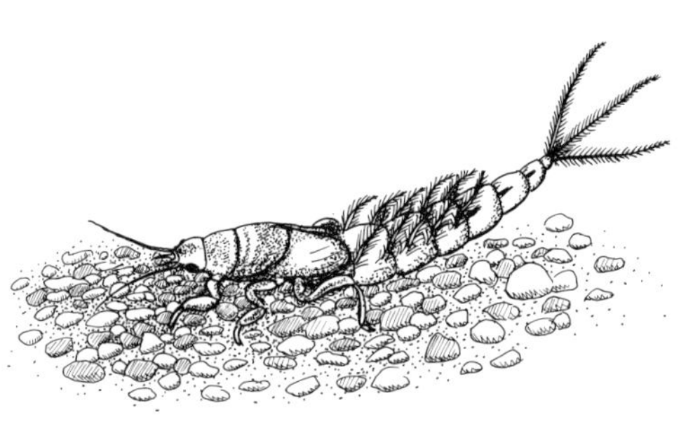

Mayfly Nymph

Muddy haunts

The mud supports other life, too. Freshwater shrimps, which were actively swimming some months ago, are now sheltering in the mud. Some water creatures produce different sorts of eggs. These can best be termed 'resting' eggs rather than the normal eggs which would hatch. Having been produced, the adults die, leaving the eggs to survive – or at least some of them – during the winter to ensure a new generation in the following year.

FISH

Some species of fish remain active during the winter, the degree of activity depending on both the species and the temperature of the water. Roach, rudd, perch, sticklebacks and pike continue to search for food throughout the winter. But they will seldom be seen, prefering to spend the time away from the surface, going deeper down where water temperatures are higher. Some species seem to take little exercise during this time of the year. Carp, tench and bream will often bury themselves in the mud, remaining there in a torpid state while conditions are unfavourable.

WATER PLANTS

Most water plants are perennials coming up each year, rather than generating new plants from seeds. They also have a way of surviving the difficult times. The water lily which graced some of our waterways last summer, is taking a well earned rest. The rhizomes, filled with food last autumn, are buried in the mud. The stored food, in the form of starch, will provide enough energy for the plant to send up shoots when conditions improve. The frogbits and milfoils have a different means of surviving. They produced winter buds which, because they are filled with stored food, sink to the bottom when the plant dies off. These winter buds will begin to germinate.

Duckweeds have an intriguing method of survival. During autumn the duckweed fronds store more food, making them heavier and they sink to the bottom. As the winter progresses some of the starch is used up so that by spring they are lighter and they will float back to the surface again.

Ponds never completely freeze over in cold weather, because of the way water behaves when it cools. Below 4°C water expands, and this is what happens when it changes into ice. Ice is lighter than water and so stays at the top. As the water near the top of the pond gets colder it stays at the here, leaving the water lower down slightly warmer. The layer of ice may get thicker as the temperature drops, but because ice is a poor conductor, no heat is lost from the lower depths.

ON THE FARM

This is generally seen as a wet month, as the old saying 'February fill dyke' seems to bear out. Although it is often the coldest statistically, weather records show that it can be the driest with the lowest rainfall – and that is probably because it's also the shortest one.

Farmers are pleased to see a layer of snow because when it covers the young corn it protects it from the cold winds and frost. If the weather is favourable some farmers will be working on the land cultivating and sowing crops. If beans haven't already been sown, they should be sown by St. Valentine's Day according to some country superstitions. Another saying suggests that unless beans are sown by St. Benedict's Day they are best left in the rick, an old word for stack, and used to rhyme with 'Benedic'.

In the past when the land was left fallow over the winter the February frosts would help to break up the soil, and this is true of any land which hasn't been planted. Some farmers will be spreading manure this month.

For some farmers many lambs will be born. Cattle are still inside and by Candlemas Day (2 February) farmers will see how winter cattle feeds are going.

'The farmer should have at Candlemas Day
Half his straw and half his hay.'

Farmers may begin to apply fertiliser to autumn sown crops, including grass when the T-sum is right – a job known as top dressing. Special machines with low ground pressure tyres will be needed if it is wet.

Winter vegetables like swedes and brocoli will be harvested, and early potatoes will be sown.

'Februeer doth cut and shear.'
'Sow cabbage when the February moon is old.'

SPECIAL DAYS

2 – CANDLEMAS DAY.

This was one of the most important days, especially as far as the church was concerned. It is dedicated to the Purification of the Virgin Mary, but was almost certainly linked to a custom of Celtic origin, known as Imbolic, and assigned to the first day of the month. Candlemas Day also has links with Roman customs too. In Celtic times Imbolic was a lambing festival, and until recently, before lambing had a longer season, the first week of February was an important time for sheep farmers who could expect the birth of their first lambs.

The term 'candlemas' derives from the custom in which a woman had to carry a candle to church when she went for her first service after childbirth. This is still observed in the Catholic Church, but was banned from the Church of England in the reign of Edward VI. The other significance of Candlemas Day is the fact that our ancestors used to light candles at this time of the year, to add strength to the sun. There are a number of sayings associated with Candlemas Day.

'If Candlemas Day be fair and bright
Winter will have another flight;
But if Candlemas Day be clouds and rain,
Winter is gone and will not come again.'

'If Candlemas Day be mild and gay
Go saddle your horse and buy them hay
But if Candlemas Day be stormy and black
It carries the winter away on its back.'

'On Candlemas Day if the thorns hang a drop
You are sure of a good pea crop.'
'Where the wind is on Candlemas Day
There it will stick to the second of May.'

14 - ST VALENTINE'S DAY.

There were two St. Valentines - and the day didn't appear to have had much importance in earlier folklore. The day is named after St. Valentine - or Saints Valentines: others would argue that the two St. Valentines are the same. The Saints lived and were martyred in the 3 century. As far as is known neither (if indeed there were two!) had anything to do with either lovers or courting couples. The link seems to be with our feathered friends. If legend is to be believed birds are supposed to find mates on the 14 February, a 'belief' which can be traced back to at least the time of Chaucer.

'This is the day birds choose their mate,
And I choose you, if I'm not too late.'

In some traditions, it is assumed that the first person of the opposite sex you meet on St. Valentine's Day will be the one you will marry. In some places young girls placed bay leaves under their pillows, on Valentine's Eve. Apparently this helped them to dream of their future husband. Some had an alternative method for encouraging a member of the opposite sex: they wore their stockings inside out. It is assumed by some people that the St. Valentine Day tradition is a revamp of the earlier Roman custom of Lupercalia, which took place in the middle of February. In spite of his popularity (at least for greeting card manufacturers, if not for every young lover on 14 February), there are no churches dedicated to the saint.

'On Candlemas Day, a good goose will lay
But on Valentine's Day, any goose will lay.'

WEATHER AND OTHER SAYINGS

'All the months in the year
Curse a fair Februeer.'

'When gnats dance in February, the husbandman becomes a beggar.'

'In February if thou hearest thunder
Thou wilt see a summer's wonder.'

'St. Dorothy brings snow (1 February).'

'Fogs in February means frosts in May.'

'Warm February, bad hay crop;
Cold February, good hay crop.'

'If snails come out in February, they will stay at home in March.'

'If cold sets in on 22 February it will last for fourteen days.'

'Saint Matthie, sends sap into the tree.'

'St. Matthew breaks the ice.'
If he finds none, he will make it.'

'If gnats hum on the last day of February,
They will be dumb for the whole of March.'

SPRING

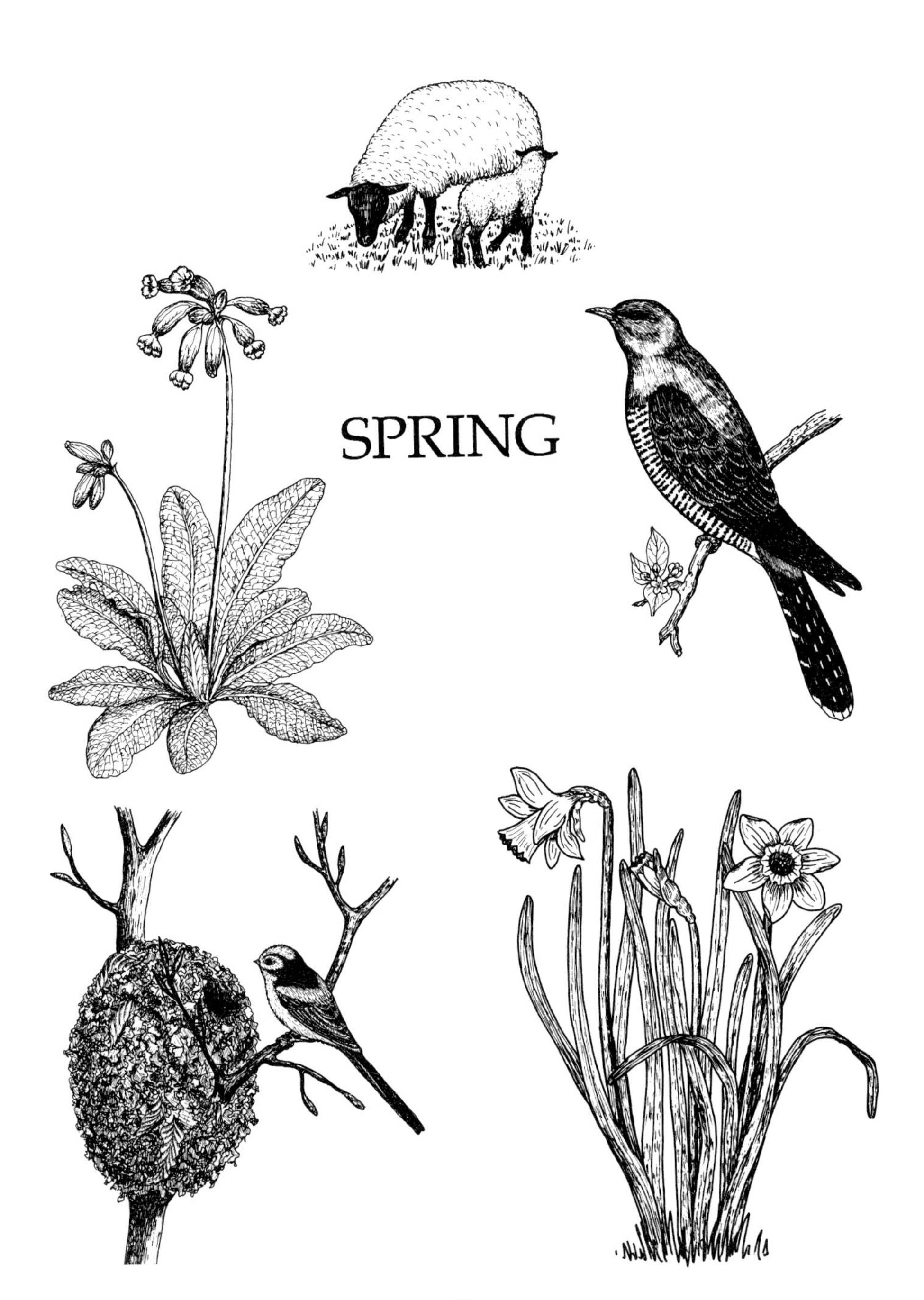

MARCH

'The sharp eyed robin hop from grain to grain
Singing its little summer notes again
As a sweet pledge of spring the little lambs
Bleat in the varied weather round their dams.'

John Clare.

Ewe and lamb

ORIGINS OF MARCH

At one time March represented the opening of the year, because in ancient times it was the first month, a tradition which was carried on by the Romans. And they named it after Mars, their god of war. It may seem strange for a month, but it was a time when hostilities could resume! They had been sporadic during the previous months because of bad weather. But now, the bringer of war needed to speed them on their way. Mars was also the god of crops and vegetation. The Anglo-Saxons had two names for the month. They called it Hyld Monath – which meant stormy month, and they also knew it as Hraed Monath – the rugged month. In Britain our year, which begins in January, wasn't a fact until the eighteenth century. Previously we had adhered to the old calendar, but in 1752 we accepted the Gregorian one, and the first of the year became the first of January.

INTRODUCTION

Everyone looks forward to March, because this is the month when we have the first day of spring. Officially it starts on the

21st to be exact. But winter doesn't just suddenly disappear on the 20 March and spring begin on the 21st. It's a gradual process. The colder weather which is usually a part of February will hopefully give rise to better days in March. It is suggested that at the Vernal Equinox on 21 March, spring advances northwards at the rate of 17 miles a day!

> *'All nature seems at work. Slugs leave their lair –*
> *The bees are stirring – birds are on the wing –*
> *The Winter, slumbering in the open air.*
> *Wears on his smiling face a dream of Spring!'*
>
> S T Coleridge

The weather will dictate, rather than the calendar, when spring has arrived. In some years it seems to come early; in other seasons it takes longer. But whatever the weather, some of the birds which have been spending the winter with us will be on their way to search for summer breeding sites.

WILD FLOWERS

With these warmer days the temperature of the ground gradually increases, and plants which have remained dormant in the soil will begin to stir. As the days of March go by, plenty should be happening in the countryside. Although we won't see too many flowers, at least at the beginning of the month, one or two new species will be joining the snowdrops and the winter aconites. The first primroses should be in flower this month.

Primrose

One other spring flower which is still quite common is the lesser celandine, a distinctive species, and undoubtedly the most noticeable of the early spring flowers which first came into bloom in February, but which will be more prominent this month. The flowers are glossy, yellow, with the petals having a delightful sheen, and arranged in a star-shape formation. The plant gets its name from the Greek which means 'swallow', and that is because flower and bird are said to appear at the same time. It was also known as swallowort in some places for that very reason. The 'Ranunculus' part of its name means 'frog', because like the amphibian, the plant also spends its life in damp places.

There are many country names for the plant including starflowers, golden stars and golden guineas. And the celandine reacts to the weather: you will find them open wide to the sunshine when the weather is fine, but closed tightly when it is dull. William Wordsworth was not only taken by the plant, so much so that he penned the following lines, but he also noticed how it reacted to the vagaries of the British weather:

'There is a flower, the
lesser celandine
That shrinks, like many
more, from cold and rain
And, the first moment that
the sun may shine,
Bright as the sun himself, '
tis out again.'

Lesser Celandine

The flower belongs to the same family as the buttercup, and with its bright flowers and supply of nectar it is a magnet for the early bees and butterflies. There is also a lovely story that swallows had need of the plant. Apparently they used the plant to cure the dim sight of their fledglings. The roots, which are said to resemble the udders of cows, were dug up at one time and hung in cowsheds.

PLANT OF THE MONTH – GROUND IVY

Ground Ivy

If the celandine is easy to spot at this time of the year, there are other plants which we probably pass by without giving them a second glance. And that is probably true as far as the ground ivy is concerned. Although it can cover some large areas because of its spreading stems and roots, it is often overlooked. But is is worth keeping an eye open for the plant.

'Pretty circlets are its leaves
Waving twins on curving stems
Finely marked with tiny veins
Daintily tucked around the hems.'

It will be coming into flower this month and next and bear blooms until June. Growing close to the ground, it is worth getting down to look at the flowers. They are deep purple and quite attractive, so I was at a loss to discover why our ancestors called them 'rat's mouth'. The leaves are an interesting heart-shape and borne on square stems with a distinctive silvery tinge.

The ground ivy isn't related to the ivy which grows on trees, but it has relatives in the same family as the mints. Apparently animals are not very keen on it, because of its spicy aroma and bitter taste. Large animals which eat it can become ill and it may cause allergic reactions in humans who come into contact with it.

But in spite of these reservations the plant was very important to our ancestors. In the days when ale was made in virtually every village, the ground ivy was collected and used to clear the ale as well as to impart a strong bitter flavour to the brew. In those days it had alternative names of 'alehoof' and 'tunhoof'. The ale bit of the first word is obvious, but the hoof is more difficult. 'Hoof' is a Saxon word for the brewing or tunning of ale. 'Tunhoof', the other alternative name, is self explanatory. Ground ivy continued to play an important part in village life until the arrival of the hop in the sixteenth century. The ale using ground ivy was subjected to a rigorous check. William the Conqueror appointed ale connors whose job it was to check the strength of the brew. As they visited the brewers, they poured samples onto wooden seats and then sat on them. If their breeches stuck to the brew it was of good quality. If they didn't then the brewer would be seriously punished.

In Georgian England when the 'sport' of cock-fighting was enjoyed by large numbers of people, ground ivy was used for curing the eyes of cocks damaged in contests. The owner picked a few leaves of ground ivy, chewed them to mix them with saliva, and then spat the liquid onto the affected bird. A similar remedy – but for human eyes – was reported by Galen from the 1st century. So convinced were people of the ground ivy's remarkable properties that they believed it would cure people with very poor eyesight.

Ground ivy was sold in the streets of London at one time because of its curative properties. People suffering from consumption also took it, as did those with asthma. Boiled leaves were made into gill tea, the liquid being drunk to cure kidney complaints, indigestion and coughs. In some places its alternative name of 'gill-by-the-ground' was a reference to this, the old name for an ale house being a gill house. But the strangest use for the plant was recorded in a book published in 1746, with the title 'A collection of above three hundred receipts in cookery, physick and surgery for the use of all good wives, tender mothers and careful nurses.' In this ground ivy was given as a cure for lunacy!

Other flowers open

The wood anemone will be in flower in woodlands. With its alternative name of 'windflower' we conjure up a picture of how the long stems sway gently in the breeze. The flower grows on a single stem and below the flower three leaves can be seen. Flowers like the wood anemone are particularly conspicuous because they appear before other woodland flowers and before the leaves appear on the trees.

Also growing in some hedgebanks will be the sweet and dog violets. According to a Greek legend the first violets sprang up where Orpheus put his lute on a mossy bank. Those who followed Bonaparte in France had the violet as their emblem because when the Frenchman was exiled to Elba he vowed he would make his return when the violets bloomed. You may also come across butterbur as well. It is later, when the large leaves appear, that the plant is particularly interesting. Butterbur grew close to many farms in the past, and the large leaves, reaching anything up to a metre across, were collected and used for wrapping up butter prior to being taken to market – before the days of refrigerated containers. Hence the plant's name. According to Gerard the butterbur might have had other uses in the past. The herbalist commented in the 16th century that the leaf 'is bigge and large inough to keepe a man's head from raine and from the heat of the sunne'.

Wood Anemone

Used by our ancestors

Butterbur plants are either male or female, and their distribution is somewhat different. Male plants occur in the southern areas, but the female flowers will generally only be encountered in more northern counties, such as Derbyshire, Yorkshire, Lancashire and Cheshire, and in some parts of Lincolnshire. In spite of this the occasional single female flower occurs amongst those which are predominantly male. From these seed is probably produced, which enables the butterbur to colonise new areas. However, it will spread to new sites close to where it already grows by using its effective creeping underground roots. Our ancestors had a use for the plant – apart from wrapping up butter. Roots were collected, ground up and then placed on spots and pimples to get rid of them.

Young unmarried girls who were desperately seeking a husband had a use for butterbur. According to tradition, they had to sow butterbur seeds half an hour before sunrise on a Friday morning, at the same time uttering these words:

'I sow, I sow
Then come my own dear,
Come here, come here
And mow and mow.'

They would then see their future husband mowing the grass, but if they were frightened or not very happy with the selection then they uttered the words 'have mercy on me' and the 'future husband' vanished. The first leaves, which usually make an effort to appear at the same time as the flowers, are far from their expansive self.

A delightful rarity

This is the month when one of he country's rare wild plants will appear. The wild daffodil, or wild narcissus, was once common in many woodlands but it has now disappeared either because of woodland clearance or because thoughtless folk decided that uprooting the plant and taking it 'back home for the garden' would be better than leaving it *in situ*. The name for the plant is very old. According to Greek legend Asphodelus was given to a plant which flourished in the meadows of the Underworld. This name is now used for a member of the lily family, but various corruptions of the original 'asphodelus' have occurred until the present day 'daffodil' arrived. The bulb yielded a narcotic which our ancestors used both as an enemetic and purgative. And in the 17th century, Nicholas Culpeper recommended it for use against all obstructions in the body. Garden daffodils are also in bloom, and Robert Herrick wrote:

'Fair daffodils, we weep
to see
You haste away so soon:
And yet the early-rising
sun
Has not attan'd his
noon.
Stay, stay,
Until the hasting day
Has run
But in the even-song;
And, having pray'd
together, we
Will go with you along.'

Wild Daffodils

Water plants

A walk in damp places can be rewarding this month, and will probably reveal the marsh marigold in bloom, yet another spring plant with yellow flowers. The 'marsh' in its name gives a clue to its preferred habitat. It has alternative names of kingcups – because of the large nature of its buttercup-like flowers. It is also known as mollyblobs. It can be found around our reservoirs, in marshy areas and also the 'damaged' edges of canals. The plant often has a long flowering period with blooms still appearing as late as June in some seasons. The name 'marigold' is a corruption of 'marygold', a reference to the Virgin Mary, and garlands of the flowers were used to brighten churches during religious festivals, and a garland was hung over the doors of houses on 1 May. Placed over cattle byres they kept evil at bay.

Other species

Some flowers continue to brave even adverse weather and yellow blooms, like those of the winter aconite and celandine may be found. The aconite closes its flowers in dull weather and opens them when it is bright. It is a poisonous species. The celandine, related to the buttercup, grows in woods and along hedgerows. The leaves are heart-shaped.

The first snowdrops appeared last month, and now, having been working under the soil for some time, more have thrown up their green leaves and their flowers continue to burst forth. The distinctive snow-white blooms add another dimension to the countryside this month.

Where there are sandy soils one plant will be showing its buds – and perhaps even the first flowers – towards the end of March. This is the moschatel, with the charming alternative name of 'town hall clock'. This name is quite appropriate and was undoubtedly coined by an observant ancestor. The five flowers are almost inconspicuous, and can easily be overlooked. Four of the flowers are arranged like the faces on a town hall clock: the fifth blossom 'stares' upwards towards the sky. Because of this it is perhaps not surprising that in the past the plant was seen as a symbol of Christian watchfulness. Moschatel takes its name from its slightly musky scent, expecially noticeable in damp weather.

TREES AND SHRUBS

Although some trees will not visibly be stirring this month, others are further advanced. Take the 'pussy' willow, the name given to the catkins of the goat willow or sallow. Here the catkins have been developing over the winter and a closer look shows two kinds. The silver ones, which give the plant its common name of 'pussy willow',are the female flowers: the golden yellow ones the male. The golden colour is due to the abundance of pollen which will be shed onto the female flowers. And they will attract many of the early insects which come because of this abundant supply of food, both nectar and pollen being produced. These insects are important because, unlike the hazel, pollination is brought about by insects and not by the wind. Bees are especially 'noisy' as they buzz and land, particularly when the weather is warm and sunny. When it is damp and cold they will be less active. Some moths will also be out of hibernation when the weather is mild and will visit the pussy willows for food.

Catkins galore

Willow Catkins (Goat Willow)

Buds continue to swell almost imperceptibly during the winter, but they are halted, albeit temporarily, when there is a cold spell. Catkins can still be seen on some hazel and also on the alder. Another tree which produces catkins at this time of the year is the aspen, although it is less well known than many other species. It is worth searching for these trees because they produce attractive catkins. The male ones exhibit a rich red colour, whereas the females are green and less attractive. A native British species, the aspen was one of the first trees to return after the retreat of the last ice age some 10,000 years ago. Where aspen occurs there are usually 'clumps' of them, with single specimens seldom being encountered. Most trees are of a single sex and this suggests that they spread by suckering.

One plant which will brighten up the scene this month is the blackthorn. The buds, safely cosseted all winter, have been straining at the leash to show what they are made of. And suddenly they make it! One day the hedge looks lifeless: the next it is bedecked with innumerable blooms of the blackthorn, even easier to see than the later hawthorn, because the leaves haven't yet appeared on the shrubs. According to tradition the flowers of the plant should never be taken into the house. But the wood was cut because it could be made into strong walking sticks. Where honeysuckle entwines the blackthorn it produces delightfully patterned wood for ideal walking sticks.

BIRDS

While visiting lakes and reservoirs it is worth keeping an eye open for the great crested grebe. These birds have already been performing their courtship displays for some while now, and even cold weather only seems to cause a slight pause to their amorous advances.

Bird activity is increasingly noticeable day by day. As the leaves begin to appear on some shrubs it will provide cover for birds like the long tailed tits which will be seeking suitable nesting sites amongst such species as hawthorn – and believe it or not – gorse. How they manage to get in and out of gorse bushes is something of a mystery. But they do, and it is quite a safe haven, preventing the attention of other species. The long-tailed tit is one of nature's superb craftsmen, and both cock and hen birds will bring the moss for the oval nest. Having completed the basic structure, the birds search for feathers to line the interior. If you can find a long tailed tit building, don't disturb it, but listen to what seems to be impatient twittering as they carry the material backwards and forwards.

Long Tailed Tit

'But the skill of some nest-building birds
is extraordinary; admirable is a fit epithet,
for the work deserves both praise and wonder.'

Lord Grey of Fallodon.

There is also an increase in the general avian chorus in March – especially as the days are ticked off on the calendar. Greenfinches will be warbling, delighting us all with their various songs. Chaffinches, robins and blackbirds will keep them company – to mention only a few. Goldcrests sing –

someone once described their trilling as 'like a wheel softly spinning'. They are said to be increasing in numbers, especially where we have a much greater acreage of conifer plantations.

Because of their numbers and conspicuous nature, you can't miss the house sparrows and they will be singing in increasing numbers this month. However, their song is hardly as endearing as some of the other species. Some sparrows, if not exactly leading the choir, have been members for some time now. But their songs are not much better than the calls they have been making through the winter.

Changes in behaviour

This is a good month to take a peek at bird behaviour. When the temperatures are low, robins will take advantage of the supply of food put out by householders. Soon, they desert this and become very territorial. Once they have their own patches, they will defend them vigorously - and fights may occur should intrusion appear irreconcilable. There is a distinctive emphasis on the song of the 'cooing' collared dove - the middle of the three coos seems to be pronounced. Birds, ready to leave us, also seem to be either happy to be going, or twitchy at the prospect. Redwings have spent the winter, feeding on our berries. They are informed by their 'body-clock' that it is time to return to Scandinavia. Blackbirds are defending their patches too.

If down below things are happening, so are things up above. Herons will probably have been mating and some will be

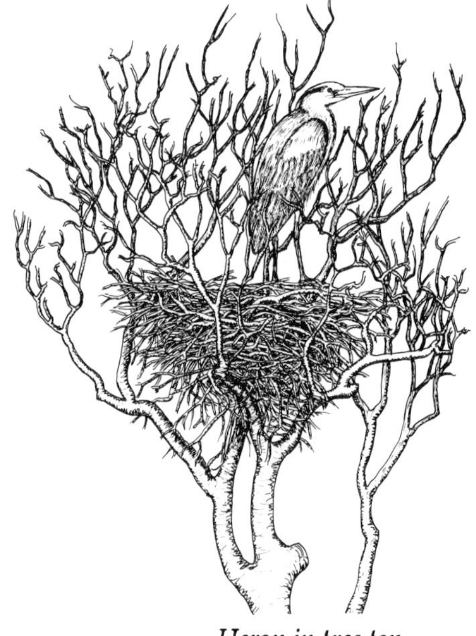

Heron in tree top

ready to lay their eggs. The treetop dance of love culminated in mating. Now the birds are sitting on their eggs, encouraging the development of the chicks. Both parents help with the chores, and as they relieve each other, they exchange a greeting with a flexing of the muscles in their long necks. He keeps guard on a nearby branch while she guards the eggs – and vice versa.

'A heron stood on one thin leg
And watched the river flow
Like a top upon its peg
He stood in the sunset glow.' Reg Scarfe.

In spite of the fact that there is time, song thrushes have already decided that the call to parenthood must be obeyed and they have started to build in bare hedges. It hardly seems worth the effort, since most of these eggs will disappear. Some may be taken by 'little boys' – in spite of the fact that it is illegal – and others by predators including jays and magpies. Here there is no sharing of duties. The male serenades the female from a suitable singing post – and also makes other birds aware of this presence. His mate sits on the nest.

BUTTERFLIES

Some butterflies may have made appearances – albeit brief – last month, and others may join them this month. Among the earliest of the butterflies to be lured out from the security of their winter's sleep, are the sulphur-coloured brimstones and an early small white may also put in an appearance towards the end of the month. Brimstones spent the winter as adults,

Brimstone butterfly

surviving the cold weather; the small white passed the winter as a chrysalid. It is interesting that butterflies were named because of the brimstones – it was the 'butter-coloured fly'. The male is a brighter yellow than the female, and after mating, brimstones lay their eggs on the leaves of either alder buckthorn or purging buckthorn. The female carefully places one egg on each leaf, selecting the underside of terminal leaves for the purpose. If more than one egg is found on a leaf then it is more likely to be the work of two separate female brimstones. Any nectar in the first flowers will provide these early emergers with a top-up of energy to keep them going or see them through a return to hibernation.

AMPHIBIANS

Water is the place for frogs. Pairs will be hanging on to each other for dear life as mating takes place. Once the eggs have been laid, and the spawn has surrounded them, they sink to the bottom of ponds and lakes. But the spawn is not on the bottom for long. Water gets into the jelly and makes it lighter, causing it to float nearer to the surface, where it will get oxygen and sunlight, necessary for development – not to mention an increase in the temperature.

According to one country tradition, frogs were useful for getting rid of toothache. You had to catch a frog, spit into its mouth, and then ask the amphibian to carry the ache away, before releasing the creature.

MAMMALS

Although hares are less common than they used to be, this month will always be synonymous with mad March hares. It is immortalised in literature, as the looney character in Lewis Carroll's 'Alice in Wonderland'. According to Pliny the name 'hare' was used because it was 'the hairiest creature of all others'. But it is possible that instead the animal got its name from the verb 'to hare', appropriate because the mammal was always being chased by hounds. It is strange how some creatures came by their 'characters' – the sly fox – the melancholic hare. But this epithet applied to the creature goes back to medieval times. It was considered a beast which suffered from bouts of depression, and it fed on certain herbs to cure its 'moods'. George Turberville, writing in his 'Book of Hunting' said, 'The hare first taught us the use of the herbe called wyld succory, which is very excellent for those which are disposed to be melancholicke. She herself is one of the most melancholicke beasts that is, and to heale her own infirmitie, she goeth commonly to sit under that herbe'. And those people who ate hares were assumed to acquire the melancholy so peculiar to this creature.

Some naturalists think that the 'March' attribute may not be accurate. It is possible that the creature was called 'marsh' hare, because it lived in these habitats. And if you live there, life is not particularly easy - and you need to keep an eye open for predatory creatures which also roam the same haunts. Moreover if perpetually chased by your foes, then it is likely that you would turn 'insane'.

Boxing matches

During spring - and especially this month - hares come together in groups and during their antics, they may participate in boxing matches. It had always been assumed that in these combats it was buck fighting buck, but recent observations show that it is generally the female attacking the male. Just before she comes on heat, a male will already have chosen her, staying close and 'shadowing' her. Sometimes she resents his attention, and turns round and as a first warning gives him a nip. If he persists in following her, she then rears up on her hind legs and lets her front feet fly! The first of such attacks will probably have taken place in the middle of February, and although they seem to reach their peak in March, hares breed right through to September. It is more noticeable in March because the fields the hare use have low-growing crops which, once they start to grow, will obscure the animals later in the year. Although seen mainly at night and at dawn, hares are also around during the day.

After mating, the female will give birth to her offspring in a surface scrape known as a form. Between one and four young are born in the open. They arrive complete with a fur coat, open eyes and are capable of moving about. Not many hours after birth, the young – known as leverets – disperse from the birth place, each seeking its own resting place. Here the young remain perfectly still until feeding time. About an hour before sunset, they will leave their daytime places and return to the birth site. The female will be waiting ready to feed them. She sits bolt upright while they take their food. This enables her to see if predators come into view. At first she spends around 8–10 minutes with each one, but within a week or so, it takes only around three minutes to feed each leveret. Having had their appetite satisfied, they will make their way to new resting places, where they will spend the next twenty-four hours. They return daily to the birth site, and the female spends increasingly shorter periods feeding them, until by the time they are four weeks old they will only take milk for a minute or so. It is not long after this, that the female's nursing care terminates, and the young are able to fend for themselves.

ON THE FARM

Where sheep are kept March is the main lambing month and this will be the main activity on such farms. What else happens will be governed by the weather. 'A peck of March dust is worth a king's ransom' according to an old country saying. Where weather permits spring cultivations will be on the increase and crops like cereals, sugar beet and peas will be sown, and potatoes planted.

Depending on the weather animals which have been in for the winter may be let out into the fields, although dairy cows may still be kept in. Milk yields begin to go down in cows which had calves the previous autumn. Some housed ewes may be put out to grass.

On farms where spring calving of dairy and beef cows is a feature the young animals will be born this month.

'A wet March makes a sad harvest.
'A warm, damp March brings muc'h harm to the farm.'

SPECIAL DAYS

LENT is a forty-day period which precedes Easter, and was a time of fasting, just as our Lord fasted in the wilderness for forty days.

SHROVE TUESDAY is the day before Ash Wednesday which marks the first day of Lent. In days gone by when fasting for Lent was much stricter than it is now, Shrove Tuesday was an 'excuse' to let off steam. All the food which couldn't be eaten during the coming fast was consumed. Shrove Tuesday is best known by its alternative name of Pancake Day. It was the custom in the past to use up the basics in the house. Making nutritious pancakes would 'stock up' the body in readiness for the fasting which was to follow. Meat was certainly banned, and although some suggest that many other foods, including eggs, were added to the list, not everyone agrees. It seems illogical to ban these, which were available to almost everyone, and at a time when the supply would be on the increase as the warmer days arrived. But perhaps banning eggs did happen. It meant that with no one able to eat them, broody hens would bring them off as the traditional 'Easter chicks' – a sign of new life in the countryside.

Other Shrove Tuesday activities included a game known as Barring-out the Master, where schoolchildren shut their teachers out of school! In one instance last century children in a school in what was then Cumberland, barricaded themselves inside the building, preventing the teachers from entering for three days!

In many places Shrove Tuesday was an excuse for taking to the streets. Processions were common in many places, and it provided an excuse for collecting for the 'poor'. During their parades, which mainly involved children, the youngsters would chant various rhymes. This one comes from Wiltshire:

'A-shrovin', a-shrovin',
I be come a-shrovin';
A piece of bread, a piece of cheese,
A bit of your fat bacon,
Or a dish of doughnuts,
All of your makin'!'

One Shrove Tuesday event which has no connection with those already mentioned, is one known as 'clipping the church'. Although celebrated on Shrove Tuesday in many places, it was also performed at other times of the year. In the ceremony children or parishioners of a particular parish gathered in the churchyard and joined hands so that they completely encircled the church. In some places, the ceremony included the singing of hymns or songs, and may also have been accompanied by a dance.

ASH WEDNESDAY. If the Shrove Tuesday celebrations were boisterous, those held the following day were of a more sober nature. This was the first day of Lent and very solemn, the name 'Ash' Wednesday coming from the blessing of ashes. It was the day on which the priest reminded his parishioners that they too will return to ashes.

But there was also a less solemn side to the day, and it was the occasion when various games were popular. Marbles - strictly for the adults - and skipping, bat and trap and tip cat were started, the climax being reached on Good Friday.

EASTER DAY is always on the first Sunday after the first full moon which occurs on or after 21 March. If a full moon is on the Sunday, then Easter Sunday will fall the following week. Which means that the earliest Easter Sunday can be is 22 March - and the latest 25 April.

PACE EGGING

Until recently this was a feature of many parts of the country, especially in northern Britain. Eggs signify new life and resurrection, and because of this featured in the Pace Egg celebrations. Painted eggs are rolled down slopes, an activity said to symbolise the rolling away of the stone from the tomb in which Christ's body was placed. The word 'pace' comes from the Hebrew for 'Passover', but the tradition has its origin in a pagan custom. Eggs were used as a symbol for the Festival of Spring, which was a time of germination and fertilisation. Many ancient peoples, including the Greeks, Romans, Persians and Chinese, all exchanged coloured eggs during their spring festival celebrations.

WEATHER AND OTHER SAYINGS

For many country folk March was described as

'The month of many weathers'

'If March comes in like a lion
It will go out like a lamb
If March comes in like a lamb
It will go out like a lion!

'A windy March foretells a fine May.'

'March in Janiveer, Janiveer in March I fear.'

'If March goes out-bone dry there'll be a bad spell of frost in late April or early May.'

'Dry March, wet May
Plenty of corn
Plenty of hay
Wet March, dry May
Little corn
Little hay.'

'On March 19 put the warming pans away.'

'March borrows its last three days from April.'

'So many mists in March,
So many frosts in May.'

APRIL

'The shepherd on his pasture walks
The first fair cowslip finds
Whose tufted flowers on slender stalks
Keep nodding to the winds.'

John Clare

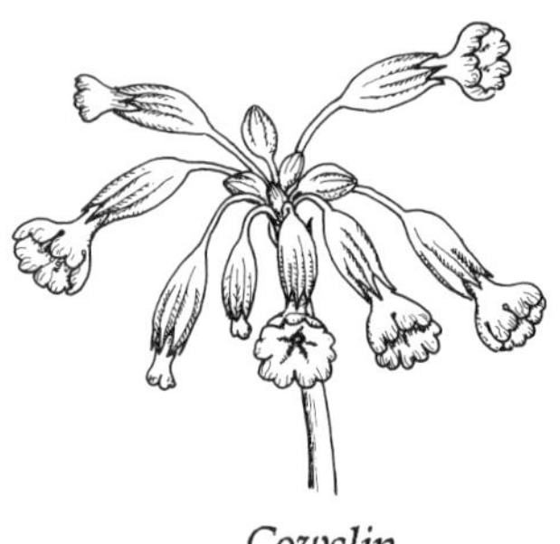

Cowslip

ORIGIN OF APRIL

April, from the Latin word 'aperire', means 'to open'. This was the language used by the Romans who dedicated the month to Venus, the goddess of love, fertility and new growth – a most apt choice! Both Greeks and Romans associated spring with the goddess Persephone or Prosperina. They believed that with the annual arrival of spring she was set free from her imprisonment in the underworld where she had spent the winter, bringing with her happiness and promoting new growth.

To the Anglo-Saxons the month was 'Eostre monath' or 'Eastremonath', and it is easy to see how the Christian festival of Easter was derived from this earlier name for April.

INTRODUCTION

Spring in the countryside signals a time for new birth and a re-awakening. Wildlife seems to sense this. Even though there will probably be cold spells in April there is 'a ray of sunshine' around the corner.

BIRDS

Birds are becoming more active this month. The songs of some of our common species liven up the countryside again. Special new sounds reach the ears this month including the unique drumming or bleating sound made by the snipe as the birds circle over their breeding grounds. This sound is produced when air passes through the bird's outstretched tail feathers, causing them to vibrate.

Snipe in flight

'..... I mine own
gain'd knowledge
should profane
if I would time
expend with such a
snipe
But for my sport
and profit.'

Shakespeare 'Othello'

Nest-building gathers momentum with more and more birds taking up the craft. Dunnocks (hedge sparrows) and blackbirds will be busy and they join other species including mistle and song thrushes which probably started last month. Now they are joined by carrion crows, magpies, and mallards. Magpies will always be associated with the rhyme

'One sorrow, two mirth,
Three a wedding, four a birth,
Five heaven, six hell,
Seven the de'il ain sell.'

In some places when a single magpie was seen, it was customary to touch the cap and

'Hullo Mr Magpie, how's your wife?'.

Blackbirds are lining the interiors of their nests with mud before the female lays her eggs. Wet weather makes nest-building easier because mud is much easier to collect.

Thrushes also finish off the inside of their nests.

'As I sit at the open window
I hear a blackbird sing
Prophetic of summer sunshine
With a song that is full of the Spring. Tas Roberts

Joyful sounds

For robins courtship started earlier in the year when they found mates and paired. Their song is particularly joyful in April. As the month progresses nest-building becomes a priority for these birds. Robins are quite adaptable when it comes to choosing nest sites, and there are many reports of birds building in unusual places, like kettles and cans. Natural sites include hedgebanks for some birds: others take to holes in either trees or walls. Ledges in sheds and outhouses may also attract the robin's attention and once a suitable site has been found the bird brings nesting materials and fashions its home here to provide a place for the eggs and chicks.

'With nests, as with plumage, we find differences
so great that they seem to be manifesting nature's—
love of infinite variety.' Lord Grey of Falloden

First of the visitors

Towards the middle of the month one of the most 'popular' summer visitors make landfall. The cuckoo will arrive if weather conditions in its winter home have been up to standard.

TO THE CUCKOO

'O blithe new-comer! I have heard,
I hear thee and rejoice.
O cuckoo! shall I call thee bird
Or but a wandering voice?

Cuckoo

While I am lying in the grass
Thy twofold shout I hear;
From hill to hill it seems to pass
At once far off, and near.

Thrice welcome, darling of the spring!
Even yet thou art to me
No bird, but an invisible thing
A voice, a mystery.' William Wordsworth

If the cuckoo's call stirs many of us there are other country folk who will be bending an ear to catch the sound of the nightingale. These birds return this month, having left us last autumn for warmer climes. Singing nightingales are seldom seen. Although they issue their melodious songs they are rather shy and retiring birds, and the opposite of 'you should be seen and not heard' applies to this summer visitor. Singing early in the morning or in the stillness of a warm spring evening, the nightingale does not attract the attention it deserves.

Nightingale numbers have decreased in recent years because one of their favourite haunts, coppiced woodland, is fast disappearing. However, recent management of certain reserves, like Glapthorn Cow Pasture in Northamptonshire, has improved conditions for this delightful species.

'The cuckoo and the nightingale
Full merrily do sing
And with their pleasant roundelays
Bid welcome to the spring
Then, care away!
And wend along with me.'

Welcome to Britain!

Apart from the cuckoo and nightingale, more than thirty other species reach our shores, including chiffchaff, whitethroat, wheatear, blackcap and willow warbler. Around five million small migrants survive the arduous journey from Africa. When spotted flycatchers arrive they eagerly search for insects to top up their energy levels. By the time they have young in the nest the supply of food should have increased to ensure that there is enough to feed the hungry nestlings. The timing varies from one season to another, and is very much dependent on the weather. On the water more and more great crested grebes are performing their courtship displays. Quarrelsome coots can be seen in combat around the edges of ponds, lakes and reservoirs, and if anything become more aggressive as spring progresses.

Countryside trees afford some protection, enticing birds seeking places for secreting their nests. Although many members of the tit family now rely on artificial nest boxes, in the natural state they search for suitable holes in trees.

'The tits they love bright colours,
Their coats are yellow-green;
That they fancy fine gay clothing
Is clearly to be seen.'

O M Bent

Noisy woodlander

The great-spotted woodpecker also needs a hole and the drilling sound is worth listening out for this month. The sound carries over a wide area especially in quiet woodlands. You may be lucky enough to hear the bird's call as well: it is a distinctive 'tchack'.

The goldcrest is our smallest bird and it may have a nest before the end of the month if the weather is good. Difficult to distinguish between cock and hen birds, he has a bill which is just a bit longer than his mate's.

Great Spotted Woodpecker

WILD FLOWERS

The tempo of life in the countryside increases in April. Flowers are coming into their own and if the saying 'April showers bring forth May flowers' is to be believed, then we should see more species next month to brighten the countryside – provided we have had the necessary rain.

The number of blooms of the yellow-flowered marsh marigold are on the increase in damp places and the plant favours the edges of ponds and pools as well as ditches and marshy areas.

Marsh Marigold

In stark contrast the white flowers of the first wood anemones were open in March, but they are particularly noticeable and make a special contribution to the April countryside. They are especially prolific in deciduous woodland as well as along hedgebanks. A shade-loving species, the wood anemone blooms under the modest shade of some broadleaved trees. The flowers of wood sorrel should be encountered in woods and coltsfoot flowers have been and gone and now the seedheads are visible, rather like the more familiar dandelion clocks.

Pin-eyed and thrum-eyed

Primroses opened some of their distinctive flower heads in March, although they will undoubtedly be at their best in many places this month. Sadly, many of our primroses have been uprooted. Primrose woods are now either devoid of these flowers, or they do not have many roots left. Primroses are worth a closer look, and you may find that the flowers are slightly different. There are two kinds of primrose flowers – thrum-eyed and pin-eyed. In the pin-eyed variety the stamens are lower down, and the styles high up. In the thrum-eyed variety, the opposite is true: the style is lower down and the stamens higher up. The reason for this is to prevent pollination by flowers on the same plant. Where you find enough primroses together about half are usually are thrum-eyed and half pin-eyed.

'And in a wood where often you and I
Upon faint primrose beds were wont to lie.'

A Midsummer's Night's Dream. Shakespeare

Primroses are sometimes collected to make primrose tea. This is supposed to cure rheumatism, migraine and arthritis. The plant is still used in homeopathic remedies. Modern remedies also make use of saponin from the root. This is one of the ingredients of expectorants in a variety of medicines.

'In a cowslip's bell I lie'

Another member of the same family is the cowslip, although it is sadly much scarcer, having vanished from many fields because of farming activities and the increased use of fertilisers and herbicides. Some cowslips still flourish in old meadows which have not been treated with herbicides. Although everyone puts the emphasis on the 'slip' part of the name, it may be that it is 'cow's lip', because the wrinkled leaves have been compared to a cow's lip.

'Where the bee sucks, there suck I
In a cowslip's bell I lie.'

The Tempest. Shakespeare

According to a legend when St Peter was told there was a duplicate set of keys to heaven, his dropped out of his hands and cowslips grew up where they fell, the flowers resembling a bunch of keys. An alternative name for the

Cowslip

plant is cowslop, because it grows where cow pats occur. The first flowers appear this month: others in May.

'The cowslips tall her pensioner's be;
In their gold coat spots you see;
Those be rubies, fairies favours
In their freckles live their saviours
I must go seek some dewdrops here
And hang a pearl in every cowslips ear.'

A Midsummer Night's Dream.

More flowers appearing

Garlic mustard, also known as jack-by-the-hedge, flourishes in April. It reaches a height of up to 120cm (24 ins) and has white flowers. The distinctive smell of garlic is experienced when the leaves are crushed. Our ancestors used garlic mustard in both spring and fish sauces. In some places it has an alternative name of 'sauce alone' for this reason.

Other flowers to look for are common violet, greater stitchwort, herb robert, cow parsley, germander speedwell, red dead-nettle, bugle, dandelion, cuckoo pint, ground ivy and ransomes. The early purple orchid should also be in evidence, in the favoured places where it still occurs.

Early Purple Orchid

TREES AND SHRUBS

Trees are beginning to reveal their leaves. Horse chestnut, beech, larch, elm, hawthorn, oak and wild cherry can be spotted, and birches have catkins. In the hedgerow, hawthorn, which will not flower until May, is overshadowed by the leafless blackthorn. The latter's flowers, many of which appeared in March, make a remarkable splash of colour like a fall of fresh snow adorning the hedgerows. Pink crab apple blossom also adds a brightness to many hedgerows and roadsides.

Blackthorn flowers

BUTTERFLIES AND OTHER INSECTS

Temperatures begin to pick up as the days in April are crossed off the calendar. Yet when the blackthorn is in flower, which may have been towards the end of last month and during April, there is often a colder spell. This is only a minor setback and in spite of it some of the more 'fragile' creatures will begin to stir. Butterflies will take to the wing. The brimstone is usually one of the first out, the earliest insects having made their appearance in March. They become particularly active in April. Later, female brimstones seek out the leaves of alder buckthorn to lay their eggs, the plant providing nourishment for the caterpillars once they hatch.

Other butterflies on the wing this month include the small tortoiseshell and the peacock. Like the brimstone, these have passed the winter as adults. Having emerged from their hibernatory quarters, one of the first tasks for all three species – brimstone, small tortoiseshell and peacock – is to recharge their batteries by seeking nectar from suitable spring flowers.

Some butterflies hibernated in the chrysalis state, and the first small whites will have made the dramatic change to adults and be ready to emerge. Moths should be around, and spring ushers are among those to be seen this month. And so it goes, the beginning of a re-awakening of life in the countryside.

Stirred into action

With a few notable exceptions, insects virtually became immobile and absent from the winter scene. Now they stir. Queen wasps usually come out of hibernation sooner rather than later. Sometimes their emergence is rather premature in an early warm spell, because if there is a return to harsh conditions they could perish. Yet those which survive will seek nourishment and a site for nest-building.

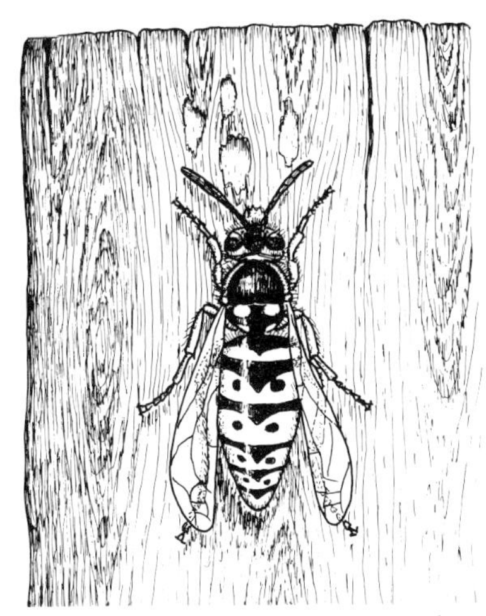

Wasp on fence removing wood

Other insects, together with a host of other invertebrates, will be out and about. Ladybirds become active as do many of the animals living in leaf litter, like millipedes and wolf spiders.

Wolf spider

And the ladybird is immortalised in the rhyme which has been chanted by country children for many centuries

'Ladybird, ladybird, fly away
home
Your house in on fire and your
children are gone.'

In my native Norfolk we used to call the creature 'bushy-bushy barnabee', which appears to be a corruption of 'bishop, bishop barnabee – when the insect is asked when a person's wedding will take place.

AMPHIBIANS

Amphibians – frogs, toads and newts – have become active. Frogs mated and spawn appeared in March. Newts and toads are also around. Toad patrols are a regular and much needed feature in several parts of the country. This service, provided by local people, is an attempt to prevent the massive slaughter of these amphibians as they cross busy roads when returning to their breeding places.

'By a quiet little stream on an old mossy bank,
Looking very forlorn, sat a little green frog;
He'd a sleek yellow back, and two bright yellow eyes,
And when dining selected the choicest of flies.'

From The Frog and the Bird by Vera Hessey

MAMMALS

Some mammals have also survived the winter by hibernating. The hedgehog is one of these and wakes from its dozy winter slumber and can be heard 'snuffling' and 'shuffling' around the garden looking for food.

'A country creature, wary, quiet and shrewd,
He takes the milk we give him, when he's gone.
At night, our slamming voices must seem crude
To one who sits and waits for silences.'

Anthony Thwaite

Bats may have been tempted out briefly on mild March days, but most which have been hanging in a 'state of suspended animation' for several months will be back in circulation some time in April. Britain provides a home to fifteen different species of bats, all of which are protected under the Wildlife and Countryside Act. Although many people believe that bats are blind this is far from the case. They have 'reasonable' eyesight, but because they are night-flying creatures have to rely on a more sophisticated insect-detecting system. In flight, each bat makes a series of rapid high pitched sounds, which cannot generally be detected by the human ear. These forward directed sounds will bounce back echoes to the bat's receiving mechanism when they hit objects in the mammal's flight path. This system not only enables the bat to

Pipistrelle

avoid crashing into objects in its way, but also helps it detect insects which will provide it with food. Each bat utters a different sound, an important consideration, otherwise bats would pick up other bats ultrasonic squeaks.

Small flying mammal

The smallest of our bats, and the most common, the pipistrelle, has a wingspan of some 9–10 inches, and because of its size it is quite often mistaken for a bird. It has an alternative country name of 'flittermouse' because of its mouse-like shape and the way it flits about. Like most other groups of mammals, bats are suffering from man's activities in the countryside. Although many species are still common, their numbers have declined, and some are in danger of becoming extinct.

MAMMAL OF THE MONTH – THE DORMOUSE

The dormouse will wake up from its winter sleep in April, having been slumbering from about last October. Once quite common it has decreased in numbers and is now a protected species. But there are encouraging signs that in some areas the mammal is making a comeback, with management techniques in some of our woodlands encouraging the creature's return. The dormouse needs woodland containing hazel, and its demise is closely linked with the decline of this

particular habitat. The mammal gets its name from its well-known habit of sleeping. In the French 'dormir' means to sleep and the dormouse is known as the 'dozy mouse' for the same reason.

Nocturnal by nature the dormouse leads a solitary lifestyle. It wakes at dusk spending the next few hours in search of food. Whereas other species of mice spend the majority of their time on the ground the dormouse carries out most of its food-gathering activities above ground level. An agile climber it is adept at moving quickly up and down creepers, such as honeysuckle and bramble. It leaps well, clearing gaps of 30cms or more.

Dormouse

Having spent almost half the year asleep the mammal loses a considerable amount of weight, in spite of the fact that its metabolic rate becomes very slow. On waking food-hunting forays are essential to the mammal so that it can build up its body weight, lost during the winter, and prepare it first for breeding and then for the period of inactivity which will follow.

Dormice in many areas have been encouraged back to some haunts which they once occupied. This has been achieved by careful management and the introduction of 'breeding' boxes. The discovery of dormice in bird boxes has prompted a study which enables various conservation groups to manage habitats to encourage these endangered mammals to return. After mating a domed nest is built in a bush often several feet above the ground. The female dormouse gives birth to between two and seven offspring any time from May to September. Sometimes two litters are born. Although they

are naked and helpless at birth they will develop a coat of grey fur, which is shed before they leave the nest when they are about a month old.

Caring for their young

Other mammals did not resort to such drastic action and hibernate. Nevertheless many have probably been less active during unfavourable weather. Badgers spent more time in their underground setts and during severe conditions grey squirrels took it easy for a day or two. But squirrels can only survive for relatively short periods without food. Now they, and the badgers, make up for 'lost time'. New generations abound undetected by most of us. Sow badgers are caring for their young below ground and female grey squirrels are nurturing their offspring not only in trees in wooded areas, but also in many solitary specimens in open countryside. Sometimes these nursery dreys can be seen moving as the females busy themselves feeding the young.

Our common red fox mated at the turn of the year and now many vixens will be nursing cubs in a special earth. Some foxes give birth as early as March; others this month, and yet more each month until July.

'Among the taller wood with ivy hung,
The old fox plays and dances with her young.
She snuffs and barks if any passes bye
And swings her tail and turns prepared to fly
The horseman hurries by, she bolts to see
And turns agen, from danger free.'

John Clare

ON THE FARM

This is the critical month for any crops which haven't already been sown because of weather conditions in previous months. Potatoes have to be in by the 15th otherwise the yields will not be high enough. Crops like kale, linseed and swedes should be sown during this month.

April can be very dry which makes it a difficult month, especially when the soil dries out. Crops need moisture to germinate and this can be a problem in dry conditions.

Farmers will be spraying fungicides, insecticides and possibly some weedkillers during April and the other spring months.

Lambing continues and the first spring lambs will appear in the markets this month. Traditionally the best prices are received at Easter. The markets will also have store cattle. These are partially grown animals which a farmer will sell on to be finished, i.e. to be fattened on grass during the coming months. All animals which have been housed for the winter should now be out of doors.

By the end of April the early rape will be in flower.

SPECIAL DAYS

1 – ALL FOOLS'/APRIL FOOLS' DAY

'The first of April some do say
Is set apart for All Fools Day
But why the people call it so
Nor I, nor they themselves do know.'

Poor Robin's Almanack of 1760

Yet in spite of not knowing why All Fools Day is celebrated, it's still a popular custom. Certain conditions have to be met, including carrying out the pranks before midday as this quote shows:

'Twelve o'clock is past and gone
And you're the fool for making me one.'

The origin of the pranks is also obscure. Some experts suggest there are connections with Lud, the Celtic God of humour. His festival was celebrated at the beginning of April.

In Scotland April Fools Day is known as 'Hunt the Gowk' or 'Gowkie Day' and bears no relation to that south of the border. A gowk is a Scottish name for cuckoo. In the Orkneys, April Fool's Day is known as 'Tailing Day' and is generally celebrated on 2 April. Pig's tails, scrounged from the local butcher, are pinned to the back of unsuspecting boys. A similar custom, called 'Tail Pipe Day' takes place at Christow in Devon on the afternoon of 1 April. A slogan like 'Please kick me' is pinned to the back of anyone who can be caught.

23 - ST. GEORGE (died about 303)

George was born of Christian parents in Cappadocia. After his father died a 'martyr's death' his mother fled to Israel with her son. He was tortured by Diolethian, where his humiliations included being covered with quicklime and having to run in red hot metal shoes.

St. George, the patron Saint of England, Portugal and Aragon, has a white banner with a distinctive red cross which forms the basis of the Union Jack.

At Filby and Hempstead, both in Norfolk, St. George is shown in the roodscreen and at Ranworth in a parclose screen. St. George is usually shown with one dragon, but an engraving of the Saint on the font at Thorpe Arnold church in Leicestershire shows him challenging not one, but two, of the beasts! The most famous legend connected with St George revolves around his dragon-killing feat. A dragon which inhabited a lake near Silene in Libya had to be given two sheep every day. When sheep became scarce young girls were fed to the beast instead. Journeying through Libya, George discovered that the King's daughter was the next maiden due to be thrown to the dragon. Not wishing to see her suffer this terrible death, George killed the dragon to save her.

The saying 'St. George to borrow' means that a farmer should be able to tell what sort of crop he can expect on St. George's Day. If his assessments are correct he can borrow money since he will have enough to repay the loan when his crops are harvested.

25 - ST. MARK'S DAY

According to historical sources St. Mark, the author of one of the Gospels in the New Testament, met his death in Egypt. His body, first buried in Alexandria, was exhumed and taken to Italy in 815AD by some Venetian merchants. Here a church was built to house his remains.

On Mark's Eve, according to legend, those living in a particular locality and who were going to die during the next twelve months took on a ghostly form and visited the local church. Legend suggests that the processions could be viewed from the churchyard between 2100 and 0100 on St. Mark's Day. The vigil has to be repeated for three years in succession. Any person who fails to keep awake dies within the year.

In parts of East Anglia those who emerged from the church would survive after having a serious illness. Anyone failing to leave the church would die. In other parts of East Anglia, including Cambridgeshire, the ghosts which left the church were the ones which would die. They walked into the churchyard to 'select' their burial sites.

PALM SUNDAY

Palm Sunday, the week before Easter Sunday, sometimes falls in April and sometimes in March depending on the date for Easter. In parts of the Midlands it is known as Fig Sunday, where a long-standing tradition says that either figs or fig pudding should be eaten on Fig Sunday.

MAUNDY THURSDAY

Maundy Thursday precedes Easter Sunday and Christians celebrate the Last Supper on that day, hence alternative names of Holy Thursday or Shere Thursday in some places. This is the day on which Christ washed the feet of the disciples and it was customary for the sovereign to wash the feet of 'inferior' people. The original practice died out, and instead Maundy Thursday became associated with the giving of money to the poor when alms were offered to poor widows. Specially minted money is distributed to the subjects, the number of people benefiting depends on the age of the monarch at the time.

Washing the feet of the poor was performed by the sovereign for many hundreds of years, James II being the last to to do this in 1658. An account of the event reads:

> *'On Maundy Thursday, April 16th, 1685, our gracious King James ye 2nd wash'd, wip'd and kiss'd the feet of 52 poor men with wonderful humility.'*

In many places a special service was held to mark Maundy Thursday and the alms distributed from the church porch, the money coming from various charities. In some areas recipients had to collect their gifts from the tomb of the benefactor so that they were aware who had provided the gifts.

The meaning of the word 'Maundy' is not clear and there are a number of theories to explain its origin. It may come from 'maund', a wicker basket used for holding earlier maundy gifts. Alternatively, it is suggested that it owes its origin to the old French word 'mande' which means a command or order. A third suggestion is that it has come to us from the old verb 'maunder' which means to beg.

The alternative name of Shere Thursday, sometimes called Shere or Chere, in other places, arises from the old tradition in which people either shaved or cut their hair in readiness for Easter Week.

Yet another explanation is that the day may have links with cleanliness, being associated with Maundy Thursday and the washing of feet. Altars were cleaned on this particular day in readiness for Easter.

GOOD FRIDAY

Good Friday is possibly a corruption of God's Friday, and until recent times it was a special day when little or no work was completed, except for essential jobs like feeding the cattle. Workers had a day off and everyone went to a special service after which they spent the rest of the day planting seeds in allotments and gardens.

Good gardeners always planted their potatoes on Good Friday because the devil was ineffective and couldn't stop the potatoes from growing.

WEATHER AND OTHER SAYINGS

A feature of April is that there is usually a colder spell in the middle of the month referred to in many places as a 'blackthorn hatch' or 'blackthorn winter', which occurs when the blackthorn blossom appears.

An upward glance at the sky often reveals small white fluffy clouds being carried above the April landscape on cold north-easterly winds while the fields below are in a frosty state.

Manx farmers have a saying which goes 'as lasting as the parching winds of spring' and in other parts of the British Isles farmers declare that once the seed has been sown it needs warm showers for germination to take place, but all it gets in a spring drought.

'April showers bring forth May flowers.'
'April weather, rain and sunshine together.'
'A windy March and a rainy April make for a beautiful May.'
'After a cold April the barns will be filled.'
'When April blows her horn it is good for hay and corn.'
'If there is thunder on April Fool's Day there will be good crops of hay and corn.'
'A cold April will bring wine and bread.'
'If April is wet there will be good wheat.'
'On Cuckoo Day (In East Sussex 14 April) it should be bright and clear.'
'A flood in April carries away both the frog and her brood.'
'April with both sunshine and showers, brings out all the wild flowers.'
'If the first three days of April are foggy
Rain in June will make lanes boggy.'
'If it thunders on All Fool's Day it brings good crops of corn and hay.'

April 3 (St. Rosamund) '...comes with the cuckoo and nightingale.'

April 4 (St. Ambrose) 'If snow falls on St. Ambrose Day then it will stay around for a further eight days.'

'On (old) Lady's Day – 6 April – the later the cold come over the water.'

'If Easter falls on St. George's Day there will be great trouble throughout the world.'

Apparently this happened in 1848, the year when Europe was rocked by revolution.

> April 25 (St. Mark's Day) *'To smell of April. May, Black Cross Day.'*

This was a reference to the black covers of crosses and relics in the procession of the Great Litany instituted by Gregory the Great in 590 AD. In parts of France the period is known as 'the days of the rosy moon'.

> *'April and May are the key to the whole year.'*

MAY

'Beneath the firdales branches dark
The little golden crested wren
Hangs up his glowing nest agen
And sticks it to the furry leaves.'

John Clare

Goldcrest and nest

ORIGINS OF MAY

It is likely that May was named after Maia, a Greek/Roman goddess whose claim to fame was that she was able to encourage growth and so increase crops. So important was she that the first of May was a special day when she was given sacrifices. Another variation is that May is named after Maia Majesta, who was the Italian goddess of spring. During Roman times, sacrifices were offered to her in the hope that she would ensure that the crop production was up to standard. Our Anglo-Saxon ancestors noticed the quickening of the pace in the countryside, and realised that as the grass grew they would be getting milk from their cows more frequently.

WILD FLOWERS

Certainly things get a move on in the countryside once May has arrived. And there is plenty to see. In several of our woods bluebells will be carpeting the ground with their delightful flowers later in the month. At one time scientists used to call the bluebell Hyacinthus non-scriptus, because they considered the scent to be similar to that of the wild hyacinth. But as the classification of plants became more careful, it was noticed that all hyacinths had a scribbling on the petals, something which was missing from those of the bluebell. The *non-scriptus* part of

Bluebells

its Latin name means 'no writing'. Its name was then changed to Endymion and the plant grouped with the lilies. As with many plants, bluebells were useful to our ancestors. The sap is very sticky, and was used as glue. Fletchers found this very useful for sticking the feathered flights onto arrows. It was also used to stick pages into books. The long leaves curl inwards and they have their uses - to the plant rather than to man. When it rains, water is 'channelled' down the centre of the leaf to the bulb, which benefits from this arrangement.

Inspirations for poets

Many of our earlier poets were eloquent about the plants of the countryside. The bluebell attracted the attention of Keats who suggested that it was 'Sapphire, queen of mid-May'. And Wordsworth suggested

'Wide as the oak extends its dewy gloom
The fostered hyacinths spread their purple bloom.'

The profusion and attractive colour of bluebell flowers, hides other interesting species which are often overlooked. One intriguing plant which intermingles with the bluebell is the greater stitchwort. It was the Victorian naturalist Richard Jefferies who took the plant to his heart. He said of the stitchwort

'There shone on the bank white stars among the grass.
Petals delicately white in a whorl of rays – light that
had started radiating from a centre and become fixed –
shining among the flowerless green.'

With its stems, reminiscent of the grasses, stitchwort has

problems standing on its own two feet as it were. It relies on the bluebells to give it support and lift its delightfully attractive head above the crowd. Producing large quantities of nectar it is a favourite with many insects. If you stand and watch stitchwort on a warm sunny day you will see a whole host of visitors, including beetles, flies, moths, butterflies, and of course those important pollinators, the bees. But in wet conditions insects will stay away, and the plant reacts by closing its flowers to the hostile weather, hanging its head, not simply in defiance, but to protect the ripening pollen.

As with many plants, the name gives away an earlier use. Our ancestors collected stitchwort, mixed it with powdered acorns and produced a brew which was used to cure a pain in the side – better known as 'the stitch'. An earlier name for the plant was 'deadman's bones' in the North of England and 'all bones' in many other places. These names were a reference to the plant's joined stems.

Less noticeable in many bluebell woods is wood avens, more correctly known as herb bennet. The plant gets its name from herbe-bene, because in past generations it was considered a cure-all. The Geum part of its Latin name means 'aromatic' and refers to the underground rhizomes, which had several uses in days gone by, including a flavouring for ale. The dark primrose-coloured flowers are in contrast to the blue of the bluebells and the white of the stitchwort.

Wood Avens

Fascinating plant

The leaves of lords and ladies – the wild arum – were very prominent in many places in April, and the unusual flower is particularly noticeable in May. It is visited by a particular species of insects known as the owl midge. They are attracted to the plant because of a decaying smell which the plant gives off: there is also an increase in temperature inside the flower which rises to some 15°C. When the insects crawl down into the flowers they are trapped by downward curving hairs. They wander around dropping the pollen already collected on visits to other wild arum plants. In bustling about inside they also collect further pollen which they will carry off with them. It seems likely that some are desperate to escape and use up excessive amounts of energy and in the process perish. The hairs wither once the flower has been pollinated and any surviving flies make their exit.

Dusted with pollen they move on to another plant where they drop their load and collect a fresh supply, ensuring that wild arum produces those distinctive, if somewhat undesirable berries, later in the year. Young men off to dances often collected a piece of the plant and carried it about their person, as they uttered:

'I place you in my shoe,
Let all the young girls be drawn to you.'

This ensured he would have the choice of all the prettiest ladies. The roots of the plants were important in days gone by. They have a high starch content, and during the reign of Elizabeth I this was used to stiffen those delightful high pleated linen ruffs which were so distinctive of this era. In Somerset, the local name for the plant was 'Jack in the green', in Northamptonshire 'Bobbin and Joan', and the 'devil's man and woman' in Shropshire.

Climbers on the move

White bryony - our only native member of the cucumber family - is producing its long trailing stems. Dismissed now as just another wild flower, it was revered by our ancestors. This was the English equivalent of the more famous mandrake. The roots were collected and the aphrodisiac qualities were supposed to have an effect on both people and horses. The female form of the plant was ground up and given to women and mares: the male variety was treated in the same way and given to men and stallions. In Lincolnshire the correct dose – 'enough to cover a threepenny piece' – had to be given to horses, otherwise there would be problems. For the Romans it had other uses. Augustus Caesar was always supposed to wear a wreath of white bryony during thunderstorms to protect him from being struck by lightning.

DOWN BY THE WATER

Common water crowfoot is in bloom and the floating leaves are different from those found below water level. This is one of nature's adaptations for survival. The below water leaves are more dissected, allowing water to pass through them more easily. Some plants have transitional leaves which show characteristics of both floating and submerged foliage. Crowfoot is a member of the buttercup family, but any 'buttercup' growing in water is a water crowfoot, although there are nine different species, which when examined closely have different characteristics.

Plant of damp places

A plant frequently found in many damp places this month is lady's smock, some of which were out last month: others will be in bloom in various places until June. The delicate mauve flowers have distinctive darker markings on the petals. To some country folk the plant is also known as 'cuckoo flower', because it blooms at the same time that cuckoos return to our shores.

'When daisies pied and violets blue,
And lady's-smocks all silver-white,
And cuckoo-buds of yellow hue
Do paint the meadows with delight.'

Love's Labour's Lost. Shakespeare

Although a common flower it was seen as the plant of the fairies and never used in decorations or brought into houses. Later when the seed pods appear the orange tip butterfly will lay its eggs, the young feeding on these pods.

By the wayside

You may still find some sweet violets in bloom this month. They grow under hedges, on banks and in woods, and possibly along the edges of meadows. And as Wordsworth noted:

'A violet by a mossy stone
Half hidden from the eye!
Fair as a star, when only one
Is shining in the sky.'

The wild pansy can also be seen in various places, including cultivated fields. Widespread herbicide use has tended to eradicate many of our once common wild flowers in some areas and the wild pansy is no exception. The field pansy is closely related to the wild pansy, but it has white flowers which are smaller than those of its relative. The plant's English name comes from the French 'pense', which means 'thought' and the pansy is always seen as a symbol of remembrance. Shakespeare had noticed the flower, and in Hamlet penned the following:

'There is pansies, that's for thoughts'.

Very much associated with love, this is epitomised in some of the alternative names which the plant has. These include 'kiss-me-quick', 'kiss-at-the garden-gate' and 'love-true'. The plant also featured in Shakespeare's 'A Midsummer Night's Dream' when Oberon took the wild pansy, and squeezed the juice into Titania's eyes, to get her to fall in love with Bottom.

'Forecasting' the weather

One species which is less common than it used to be is the scarlet pimpernel, and it is worth searching for and is certainly an attractive species. The flowers are only open from around 8am to 3pm, and they remain closed on dull and wet days. In fact it used to be known as 'poor man's weatherglass' because the flowers opened and closed depending on the weather. It was an important plant for the herbalists, since it was supposed to dispel melancholy and cure madness. It is also said to give 'second sight' to anyone upholding it. If it is dropped into moving water, scarlet pimpernel is supposed to move against the current. Naturally Gerard noticed the plant, but why he wrote,

> *'No heart can think, no tongue can tell,*
> *The virtues of the pimpernel.'*

is a mystery.

Scarlet Pimpernel

More plants to find

Watch out for meadow and bulbous buttercups, common fumitory, dovesfoot cranesbill, deadly nightshade, silverweed and horseshoe vetch. Fumitory produces nectar, but it doesn't appear to be attractive to insects, and the plants are generally self-pollinated. The word 'fumitory' comes from the Latin meaning 'smoke of the earth'. When you pull a fumitory plant from the soil, the roots give off a smell which is reminiscent of nitric acid, and it is for this reason that the Americans have named the fumitory 'fume plant'. The 'smoke' attribute is also noticed if the sap gets into the eyes: it makes them water in a similar way to smoke getting into eyes. Although the

Deadly Nightshade

plant does not appear particularly attractive, the pink flowers are worth a second glance, because they have dark tips.

TREES AND SHRUBS

Hedgerows are improving by the day, with plants living there making good headway. Hawthorn will be in blossom and the white flowers add a delightful splash of colour.

'When the hawthorn bloom too early shows,
We shall have still many snows.'

or as John Milton said

'....every shepherd tells his tale
Under the hawthorn in the dale.'

To talk about hawthorn is a bit misleading since there are two species. The Midland hawthorn is, as the name suggests, mainly confined to Midland counties. The common hawthorn is much more widely distributed. It is understandable that because of its links with spring, the hawthorn played an important role in earlier folk customs. On May day sprigs of flowers were hung outside the cowshed, to ensure a continuing supply of milk. Before 1752, Northamptonshire folk planted hawthorn branches outside the home of the prettiest girl in each village.

Hawthorn in folklore

The Green Man was as much a part of this season as the hawthorn and in many cases the two were inseparable, with the green man wearing a wreath of hawthorn. If you worked as a servant in Suffolk you always searched for a branch of flowering hawthorn on May day. Taken to the master of the house it would be exchanged for a dish of cream for breakfast. To keep a house safe a May branch was collected and placed in the rafters on Palm Sunday or Ascension Day. The rituals have long been recorded and in 1350, Sir John Mandeville notes:

Hawthorn

> *'And therefore hath the white thorn many virtues.*
> *For he that beareth on hym thereof, none manner*
> *of tempeste may dere him: be in the hows that yt*
> *is ynne may non evil ghost entre'.*

And a popular rhyme was known in many counties:

> *'Beware of an oak,*
> *It draws the stroke,*
> *Avoid an ash,*
> *It courts the flash,—*
> *Creep under the thorn,*
> *It will save you from harm.'*

When the calendar was changed in 1752, it meant that hawthorn came into flower later than the first day of the month.

But it wasn't only the flowers which were sought after. It was believed that anyone who bathed in the dew of the hawthorn on May morning would improve and retain their beauty, an act which the wife of the famous diarist Samuel Pepys performed in 1667 according to an entry in his diary. The following rhyme testifies to the value of such an activity:

'The fair maid who the first of May,
Goes to the field at the break of day
And washes in dew from the hawthorn tree
Will ever after handsome be.'

Some country folk still comment on the way in which fruits foretell the sort of weather we can expect. In a Norfolk Garland published in 1872, it is stated that:

'Many haws, many sloes
Many cold toes.'

A show of leaves

Catkins have already been on hazel, alder and willow earlier and now the leaves will be making good progress. The silver birch is slightly different: catkins and leaves appear together. Sycamores have their leaves, the black buds of ash are swelling and opening and beech is on the move.

Silver Birch Catkins and Leaves

It is from the hazel that twigs used in divining are taken. For the rod to be effective, it had to be cut on St John's Eve or Night. And interestingly until about the 1700, the twigs were also supposed to be capable of pinpointing thieves as well as water. In many places a band of hazel was woven and placed round the breast of a horse to protect the creature from fairies. In Celtic times a small twig was cut and kept in a house to protect it from lightning.

In many areas the hazel has been important in the countryside. Hazel coppice features in many woodlands, the material being used for thatching. In other places areas of hazel was coppiced to produce a regular crop of hazel or cob nuts. According to a Midland saying:

'Many nuts – many pits (graves).'

But as with so many of these country sayings by contrast, in other places, a good crop of nuts was said to foretell a good crop of babies.

INSECTS

May is the month when mayflies will be out – as their name suggests. The female laid her eggs in water perhaps as long as three years ago. In May the nymphs are ready to leave the water. In fact some may already have emerged towards the end of April. But most will be on the wing in May. The mayfly has a unique life cycle as far as insects are concerned. In the water the larval form spent most of its time burrowing in soft mud at the bottom of a stream where it fed on small water life known as diatoms and probably taking other kinds of algae as well. Ready to leave the water, the nymph makes it way up the stem or onto a stone. A winged form then emerges. This flutters off and rests on a plant. In fact this isn't the adult, but is known as the dun, which is a favourite with the angler. Although this stage resembles the adult which it will shortly turn into, it is characterised by its opaque, dingy wings. The life of the adult mayfly will be short. Most will have mated and be dead within a few hours, although others may live for three or four days.

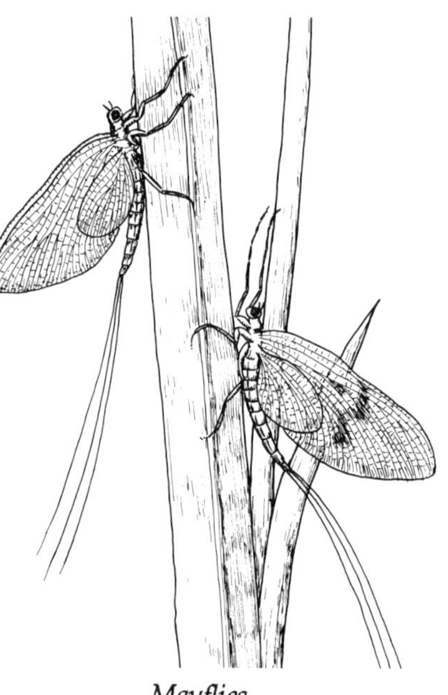

Mayflies

On a warm spring evening it is a delight to watch the clouds of mayflies as they rise and fall during their mating flights. The females need to lay their eggs in water and these flights take place close to aquatic environments. There are many different species: some are quite common; others much rarer. One of those most often seen is one of the largest. Known as Ephemera danica, it has a wingspan of nearly 25mm (2ins), and the characteristic trailing tails.

Harmless maybugs

Another creature named after the month in which it is active is the maybug, properly known as the cockchafer. These beetles cause quite a stir when they enter houses. They are large, some 3cm (1.25ins) long, and are attracted to lights. In older houses the insects fall down chimneys, making a lot of noise as they do so, fluttering about in their attempts to escape. But in spite of their size they are harmless. Although the adults are of little consequence the same cannot be said for the larvae. Adult female cockchafers lay their eggs in the soil. Once these hatch, the larvae feed on a variety of plants including trees and shrubs. As they grow they increase in size reaching a maximum length of around 60mm (2ins) and a thickness about that of a small finger. The white body, which has a brown head equipped with powerful jaws, is not unlike corrugated paper. As in other insects there are three pairs of legs, although these are not particularly powerful.

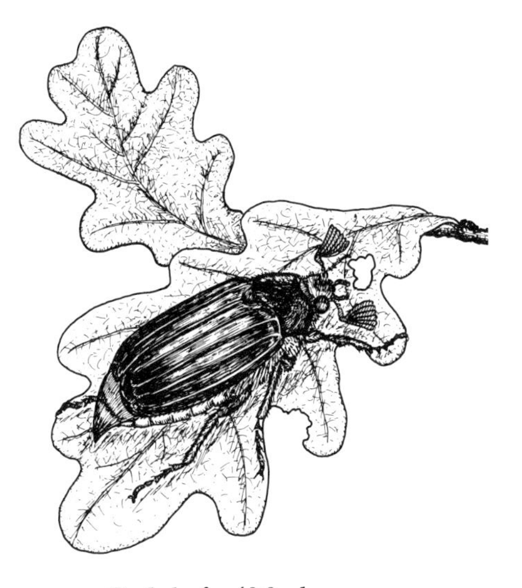

Cockchafer / Maybug

Soaking up the sun

Other insects are on the wing, and butterflies take advantage of the sun. Several species use walls as radiators. The small tortoiseshell often lands here, spreading its wings to soak up the warmth. You may also see the meadow brown doing the same thing. The female of the species will be looking for grasses on which to lay her eggs. She is not fussy about the particular species, and once she has found a plant she places her eggs singly on the leaves.

Orange tip butterfly

The orange tip butterfly will be on the wing this month, having spent the winter in the pupal form – which somewhat resembles a miniature boomerang. Of the two sexes, it is the male which will emerge from hibernation first and it is only he which sports the orange tips to the wings. As with many other creatures, this is a warning to predators to beware: the orange tip doesn't have a pleasant taste. However, such evasive tactics don't put off every creature, and undoubtedly many orange tips will fall prey to a variety of species.

The females appear a week or so after the males – depending to some extent on weather conditions. Having made her appearance the female tends to stay fairly close to the plants on which she will lay her eggs. Apart from lady's smock she will also seek out other crucifers. Egg-laying is vital to ensure that there will be another generation of orange tips, and she places a single egg on each plant. The reason for this is not known, but it is seen by many entomologists as a survival feature. A single egg means that predators have to search hard. It could also be due to the fact that once the caterpillars hatch they are said to be cannabilistic and might devour their 'brothers' and 'sisters'!

Active insects

It is worth watching cow parsley in the hedgerows. Hoverflies will come to feed on the lovely umbrella-shaped flower heads. Ants will be around, under and above ground caring for the young once the eggs hatch. Having found suitable sites wasps will be busy nest-building and expanding them as the workers develop and take over the job.

Bees are hard at work collecting nectar and pollen. The large queen bumblebees will have found some food last month. But now the choice and quality increase. It is intriguing watching the heavily laden bees with full pollen baskets making their way back to the nests. Soon the workers will emerge, and the queen will have less work to do – except to continue to lay eggs. Other wild bees, including the cuckoo bees, will be abroad. These parasitise the nests of the bumblebees. They seem to survive the first onslaught and attacks which any intruder must get, and the female cuckoo bee eventually settles in to lay her own eggs.

BIRDS

There are plenty of signs that birds are especially active. Some have obviously been busy working for a couple of months now. But of course May marks a greatly increased tempo for these wild feathered and fascinating neighbours. Many of our 'spectacular' summer visitors are busy, with swifts, swallows and martins nest-building. They are all extremely accomplished aerobats, but probably none can match the swift for its manoeuvres.

Swift (viewed from underneath)

Swallows are having greater difficulty in finding nesting sites, which seem to decline in numbers each year. They are particularly interested in buildings like barns and outhouses with 'rafters'.

You should be able to see spotted flycatchers and linnets: they ought to have found suitable nesting sites. The latter often look to gorse bushes for somewhere to build. It is worth listening out for the male linnets as they let forth a series of 'twittering' notes and reed buntings will be looking for marshy areas in which to nest. They have expanded their habitats in recent times, perhaps because of the disappearance of much marshy terrain. Sewage farms have become attractive sites and they also build nests in grass tussocks and they are not averse to placing them in osiers. Once the nests are woven they may add a reed flower as final decoration.

BIRD OF THE MONTH – THE WREN

One of Britain's smallest birds is building a distinctive nest this month. The wren is only beaten to the record by the goldcrest which is a quarter of an inch smaller. For its size it has also got one of the most delightful songs, and that, coupled with its jaunty approach and cocked up tail, and for such a small bird its manner almost seems like an act of defiance. And the bird has certainly been respected for a long time.

Both cock and hen birds have come to be known as 'Jenny Wren' – and that has undoubtedly happened because it is difficult to distinguish between the two. The male has been busy for a little while now. He needs to attract a mate. And his way of doing it is quite unusual. Instead of producing one nest, he builds several from which the female selects the one of her choice:

Wren

'Or in sequestered lanes they build
Where, till the flitting bird's return,
Her eggs within the nest repose,
Like relics in an urn.' Wordsworth 'A Wren's Nest'

Having laid her first batch of eggs and hatched the chicks, the cock bird may take these away to one of the unused nests because the female often produces a second clutch. It may be that in areas where there is plenty of food the male may entice more than one female to his homes. But if there is a scarcity of edible matter he will only use one nest.

Severe winters cause problems for wrens. Being such small birds they quickly lose a large amount of body heat in cold weather. To keep warm many wrens cluster together in nestboxes and in holes in trees – almost anywhere which will keep them warm. Even here some of those on the outside may perish, with those in the centre of the roosting site coming off best.

MAMMALS

There will be plenty of activity in wooded areas. Below the ground some vixens have cubs which are growing apace. It is worth watching at a fox's earth when the cubs are between 3–4 weeks old. You do need to take precautions, ensuring that your scent doesn't reach the earth. If it does the foxes become suspicious and will probably not 'perform' for you. These earths may not be too easy to find, because they are generally well hidden in places where woodland vegetation is growing well. However, the activity of the adults and young does lead to a trampling down of the plants close to the earth.

The cubs start to move above ground at this time – aided and abetted by the vixen – where they start their playful sessions and can become quite active. But the vixen is still in charge. One sharp bark from her and they 'toe the line', scurrying back into the earth as fast as their legs will carry them. Having been fed on the vixen's milk she now has to get them on to solid food. A supply of small mammals, especially young rabbits, seems to tempt them as she weans them on solids just like the human mother. Birds will also be captured by the adults and offered. But the cubs have some way to go before they are self sufficient. It will be July before they are capable of sustaining themselves by capturing all their own food.

If there was a mild winter with a dry spring then many of the small mammals 'jump on the bandwagon' and will already be rearing their young. This means that they can go on producing new litters as the year progresses. There seems to be a controlling factor in that food supplies – and later the weather – will determine how many of these young survive. The casualty rate may be high, and the number of youngsters reaching maturity no more than in a poor season when breeding starts later. But with all these small mammals around – voles, mice and shrews – other creatures have less trouble finding food. Birds of prey have a ready-made meal and carnivores also take their share.

Shrew

Active urchins

Hedgehogs are now very active after the winter's rest. Not that long ago they were known by the alternative names of urchin and hedgepig. These prickly mammals are scouring hedgerows and gardens for a supply of food. They are very good at controlling the pest population at this time. They take grubs, slugs and other creatures which might cause damage to plants. Some of last year's late offspring have difficulty finding enough food before they hibernate, and may not survive the winter. But if they do the adult hedgehog population will be greater the following year.

Breeding takes place this month, although some will have mated already and there will be pregnant females around. As far as the hedgehogs are concerned they hardly keep their courtship rituals a secret. These are noisy affairs with much grunting and squealing. Males may circle females for considerable periods of time – and even then one or other may scurry off quite unexpectedly, the encounter resulting in nothing. It is not unusual for more than one male to attempt to woo a female. But any males which try to win the female are generally seen off by the first male. There are times, however, when the new arrival will beat off the earlier suitor and endeavour to engage the female's attention.

Large numbers of these mammals seem to come to grief on roads this month, as they search for new territories and mates. Many of these will be last year's youngsters. If you have hedgehog visitors to your garden they leave black cigar-shaped droppings on lawns and paths. They are more common in gardens than many people suspect – and are frequent visitors to urban flower beds.

Reptiles will be around, and grass snakes can often be seen swimming in ponds, lakes and streams, where they find food. As the month gets warmer they seem to spend more time sunning themselves.

ON THE FARM

The most noticeable activity this month is silage making. This is the start of the period when farmers will store grass to be used as feed next winter. The best silage is said to come from grass which is cut and then allowed to wilt slightly. It is then chopped and put into some form of sealed 'container' – it may be a tower silo, clamps or plastic 'bags'. Recently wrapping machines have been developed which enable the farmer to wrap small quantities of grass for silage. It is important that air is excluded so that, as the grass ferments, acid is produced which preserves the grass. As grass is cut and removed, slurry – liquid manure which is produced during the winter months – will be spread on the fields to encourage re-growth.

Maize, which is grown for silage, can't be sown until after the last frosts at the beginning of May. It is one crop which is often grown in the same field year after year.

Shearing, which begins this month and goes on until July, covers a longer period than in the past because the contractors who are used have to travel from farm to farm. The wool needs to be removed from the sheep but at present there is a world glut and prices are low.

This month the weather may be humid and this causes problems with flies, and sheep have to be treated now and throughout the summer against these and other external parasites, and also dosed to control internal parasites.

Some of the beef cattle which were turned into the fields in spring will now be ready for market.

Spraying to control weeds on a variety of crops takes place. In the past sugar beet for example, was hoed to keep the weeds down. This was labour intensive and time consuming. Spraying has cut down the costs. Other controlling sprays, such as fungicides and insecticides, are being used.

Although some rape was in flower last month, traditionally this is the month to see the yellow fields across the countryside.

In parts of the country where conditions are right, the first new potatoes may appear in May.

Orchards will be in blossom and the bees will be out on their rounds to ensure that pollination takes place and the seeds are set so that fruit will be produced.

SPECIAL DAYS

MAY DAY

From time immemorial May Day has been celebrated as a spring festival, and although we celebrate it at the beginning of the month, before the change of calendar in 1752, it was eleven days later, when spring would have been more advanced and the frosts predicted during the Ice Saints Days would have passed.

Our pagan ancestors celebrated the return of growth to the countryside. Seeds which had been planted a short time ago were pushing through the soil. As far as animals were concerned, farmyards – and most backyards – were alive with the sound of new born chicks, and in the fields, lambs could be seen.

On May Day our ancestors turned their attention to the greenwood and young people went 'a-mayin', and brought back greenery the following morning – to celebrate nature's revival. They went back to the village, decorating doors and windows with the greenery they had collected in the greenwood. They also blew horns, a custom started during Julius Ceasar's reign, to herald the summer.

A pine or birch tree stripped of its branches was carried back to become the maypole, a custom which has its origins in pre-Christian Roman mythology, where Kybele was the goddess of flowers and of fruitfulness.

The May Day festival stayed as part of the calendar for many centuries, until Oliver Cromwell banned all festivities, though they were later revived by Charles II. Everyone enjoyed themselves from the monarch down to the humblest of servants.

Maypoles have always been brightly decorated and festooned with flowers, but the ribbons which we associate with the maypole and the dancing, are a relatively recent innovation. They arrived from the Continent in the nineteenth century. The ribbon plaiting dance is also 'modern'.

Although some maypoles became famous and stayed in situ for many years most were taken down and used either for ladders or for house beams. A ladder in the belfry in Castle Bytham Church in Lincolnshire has the words 'This was the May Poul 1660'.

Another important May Day activity was the crowning of the May Queen and May King – or the Green Man. This custom is believed to be associated with the Kybele-Attis traditions. The ceremony included a mock marriage which symbolised the joining together of all living things – and signified fertility.

29 - OAK APPLE DAY
is kept to mark Charles II's triumphant entry into London in 1660. To commemorate this event oak twigs and leaves were worn: houses and horses were also decorated. In Northampton it is the custom to decorate the statue of Charles II over the portico of All Saints Church. The King gave the town wood after a disastrous fire.

WEATHER AND OTHER SAYINGS

May is certainly well known for two weather sayings,

'Don't cast a clout 'til May is out',

which has always caused a great deal of debate. Does it means the month, or does it mean hawthorn - known as may by country folk? The other is:

'March winds and April showers bring forth May flowers'.

But in recent times when we have had topsy-turvey weather it's no longer possible to predict this!

A wet May is also said to bring a good load of hay. This simply means that there should be enough sun in June to ripen the grass.

May 11 is the feast day of St. Marmertius, the 12 St. Pancras and the 13 St. Gervais, who collectively are known as the 'Ice Saints', because these three days usually bring morning frosts, which is said to be 'winter having its last kick'.

If it rains on St. Urban's Day, the 25 May, then

'every ear of corn loses a grain'.

Apparently the Saint also

'gives the summer'.

If it rains on St. Philip (of Neri) day, the 26 May, then 'the poor man has no need to beg of the rich man'. This suggests that there will be good crops - and plenty for all.

INDEX

Books Published by THE BOOK CASTLE

CHANGES IN OUR LANDSCAPE: ASPECTS of BEDFORDSHIRE, BUCKINGHAMSHIRE and the CHILTERNS, 1947–1992: from the photographic work of Eric Meadows. 350+ fascinating colour and monochrome pictures by the area's leading landscape photographer. Detailed introductions and captions.

JOURNEYS INTO HERTFORDSHIRE: Anthony Mackay. Foreword by The Marquess of Salisbury, Hatfield House, Nearly 200 superbly detailed ink drawings depict the towns, buildings and landscape of this still predominantly rural county.

JOURNEYS INTO BEDFORDSHIRE: Anthony Mackay. Foreword by The Marquess of Tavistock, Woburn Abbey. A lavish book of over 150 evocative ink drawings.

NORTH CHILTERNS CAMERA, 1863–1954: FROM THE THURSTON COLLECTION IN LUTON MUSEUM: edited by Stephen Bunker. Rural landscapes, town views, studio pictures and unique royal portraits by the area's leading early photographer.

LEAFING THROUGH LITERATURE: WRITERS' LIVES IN HERTFORDSHIRE AND BEDFORDSHIRE: David Carroll. Illustrated short biographies of many famous authors and their connections with these counties.

THROUGH VISITORS' EYES: A BEDFORDSHIRE ANTHOLOGY: edited by Simon Houfe. Impressions of the county by famous visitors over the last four centuries, thematically arranged and illustrated with line drawings.

ECHOES: TALES and LEGENDS of BEDFORDSHIRE and HERTFORDSHIRE: Vic Lea. Thirty, compulsively retold historical incidents.

LOCAL WALKS: NORTH and MID-BEDFORDSHIRE: Vaughan Basham. Twenty-five circular walks, each linked to an interesting topic.

LOCAL WALKS: SOUTH BEDFORDSHIRE and NORTH CHILTERNS: Vaughan Basham. Twenty-seven thematic circular walks.

CHILTERN WALKS: BUCKINGHAMSHIRE: Nick Moon. In association with the Chiltern Society, the first of a series of three guides to the whole Chilterns. Thirty circular walks.

CHILTERN WALKS: OXFORDSHIRE and WEST BUCKINGHAMSHIRE: Nick Moon. In association with the Chiltern Society, the second book of thirty circular walks.

COUNTRY AIR: SUMMER and AUTUMN: Ron Wilson. The Radio Northampton presenter looks month by month at the countryside's wildlife, customs and lore.

COUNTRY AIR: WINTER and SPRING: Ron Wilson. This companion volume completes the year in the countryside.

WHIPSNADE WILD ANIMAL PARK: 'MY AFRICA': Lucy Pendar. Foreword by Andrew Forbes. Introduction by Gerald Durrell. Inside story of sixty years of the Park's animals and people – full of anecdotes, photographs and drawings.

FARM OF MY CHILDHOOD, 1925–1947: Mary Roberts. An almost vanished lifestyle on a remote farm near Flitwick.

SWANS IN MY KITCHEN: The Story of a Swan Sanctuary: Lis Dorer. Foreword by Dr Philip Burton. Tales of her dedication to the survival of these beautiful birds through her sanctuary near Hemel Hempstead.

A LASTING IMPRESSION: Michael Dundrow. An East End boy's wartime experiences as an evacuee on a Chilterns farm at Totternhoe.

EVA'S STORY: CHESHAM SINCE the TURN of the CENTURY: Eva Rance. The ever-changing twentieth-century, especially the early years at her parents' general stores, Tebby's, in the High Street.

DUNSTABLE DECADE: THE EIGHTIES: – A Collection of Photographs: Pat Lovering. A souvenir book of nearly 300 pictures of people and events in the 1980s.

DUNSTABLE IN DETAIL: Nigel Benson. A hundred of the town's buildings and features, plus town trail map.

OLD DUNSTABLE: Bill Twaddle. A new edition of this collection of early photographs.

BOURNE AND BRED: A DUNSTABLE BOYHOOD BETWEEN THE WARS: Colin Bourne. An elegantly written, well-illustrated book capturing the spirit of the town over fifty years ago.

ROYAL HOUGHTON: Pat Lovering. Illustrated history of Houghton Regis from the earliest times to the present.

Specially for Children

ADVENTURE ON THE KNOLLS: A STORY OF IRON AGE BRITAIN: Michael Dundrow. Excitement on Totternhoe Knolls as ten-year-old John finds himself back in those dangerous times, confronting Julius Caesar and his army.

THE RAVENS: ONE BOY AGAINST THE MIGHT OF ROME: James Dyer. On the Barton hills and in the south-east of England as the men of the great fort of Ravensburgh (near Hexton) confront the invaders.